FATAL DUTY

The Scottish Police Force to 1952:
Cop Killers, Killer Cops & More...

GARY KNIGHT

With illustrations by **ROB HANDS**

TIPPERMUIR
· BOOKS LIMITED ·

Fatal Duty. The Scottish Police Force to 1952:
Cop Killers, Killer Cops & More...
A Gary Knight Book. Copyright © 2021. All rights reserved.
The right of Gary Knight to be identified as the author of the
Work has been asserted in accordance with the
Copyright, Designs & Patents Act 1988.

This first edition published and copyright 2021 by
Tippermuir Books Ltd, Perth, Scotland.
mail@tippermuirbooks.co.uk – www.tippermuirbooks.co.uk.

ISBN 978-1-913836-05-4 (paperback)
A CIP catalogue record for this book is available from the British Library.

Editorial and Project coordination by Dr Paul S Philippou.
Cover design by Rob Hands and Matthew Mackie.
Editorial support: Jean Hands and Steve Zajda. Illustrations by Rob Hands.
Text design, layout, and artwork by Bernard Chandler [graffik].
Text set in Plantin Std 10.2pt on 15pt with Clarendon BT titling.

Frontispiece: Nineteenth Century Sergeant of Police, and Police Officer
(*Perth Museum & Art Gallery*)

Printed and bound by CPI Group (UK) Ltd, Croydon CR0 4YY.

Acknowledgements

Behind every published book is a team without whom the book would not see the light of day. *Fatal Duty* is no different in this regard. From the very beginning, my wonderful wife, Lynne, took on a larger than fair proportion of household duties, so that I could concentrate on research and writing. Not only did she allow me to sit upstairs in peace and quiet for hours on end, but she also gave constant encouragement to my efforts.

As a result of dyslexia, my writing is too much sometimes even for the best computer spellchecker. Luckily, I had help from Andrea Campbell, to whom I offer thanks. She proofread the manuscript before its submission to my publishers.

A very big thanks to all at Tippermuir Books Limited: Paul Philippou for his support and involvement throughout the book, Rob Hands for his illustrations, Matthew Mackie for the cover, Jean Hands and Steve Zajda for their proofreading, and Bernard Chandler for his layout. Thanks also go to Paul Adair, the photographic officer at Perth Museum & Art Gallery, for his help in sourcing images for the book.

Also by Gary Knight from Tippermuir Books:
NO FAIR CITY
DARK TALES FROM PERTH'S PAST

A QR code that links to Gary's History and Horror Tours Website:
https://www.historyandhorrortours.com/

Contents

Foreword

In the past, law and order would have been the responsibility of local sheriffs and magistrates, acting on behalf of the monarch. Armed town guards patrolled streets and manned city walls and gates. In addition, church officials could try, condemn and punish members of the population, usually for perceived moral misdemeanours.

The major cities of Scotland were volatile places whose disaffected citizens would often riot. Unpopular laws, food shortages or responses to botched executions often led to disorder. If a town or city guard could not control matters, the army might be called out to restore order. The use of troops in these situations often ended tragically. In Edinburgh, in 1736, the hanging of a popular smuggler led to a celebrated disturbance known today as the Porteous Riot in which the captain of the city guard, John Porteous, ordered his troops to fire on the unarmed populace resulting in six deaths.

Some sixty years later, on 29 August 1797, during demonstrations against the conscription element of the Militia Act 1797, troops not only fired on a crowd of demonstrators, but they also ran amok killing and wounding people not even involved in the demonstration. This event became known as the Massacre at Tranent. Five years later, troops fired into a crowd in Aberdeen, killing three and injuring many more. In order to forestall revolt against these acts of state violence, the authorities recognised that an unarmed force was needed to police Scotland's cities.

City constables acted as night watchmen and patrolled the nation's streets. These city constabularies evolved into a policing force. The force set up in Glasgow in 1779 became the first professional police force in history. From the outset, it struggled due to a lack of finance. The Glasgow Police Act 1800, which tasked the police force with keeping order in the rapidly growing city changed matters. Other cities followed: Edinburgh in 1805 and Aberdeen in 1818. In a similar manner, Burgh and shire police forces serviced the smaller towns and outlying countryside.

It became clear that policing was a dangerous task. The first police officer to die while on duty was Dugald Campbell in Edinburgh 1812. More recently, in 2019, Constable Roy Buggins collapsed while directing traffic in Montrose. On the same day that I visited the police college at Tulliallan Castle to take a photograph of the memorial to the officers killed on duty in Scotland (22 September 2020), Sergeant Matt Ratana was shot dead in London,

Fatal Duty details those police officers killed while on duty through acts of violence or in accidents from 1812 to 1952; and those, where known, who were responsible for their deaths – 'Cop Killers'. The time period covered by this book is one in which policing was at its most perilous: constables patrolled alone and at night with only a wooden baton for protection and a whistle to attract assistance if attacked. This is a time before police patrol cars, radio, helicopters, drones, armed response units, riot police and specialised equipment became everyday resources. The book also includes those police officers whose actions, be they accidental or murderous design, resulted in killing – 'Killer Cops'.

Policing is still a dangerous job. I would like to dedicate this book to all those police officers who have made and make our cities, towns, villages and streets safer.

Gary Knight
March 2021

PART ONE

Cop Killers

I
Police Watchman Dugald Campbell
Edinburgh City Police

3 January 1812

WHEN WORK started on the New Town of Edinburgh in 1767, it became clear that the elegant new buildings, wide leafy streets, and tasteful green spaces would function as a magnet for the well-to-do. This new development would pull the monied elite from the stinking, decrepit, overcrowded old town down the hill and across now partly drained Nor Loch.

OLD TOWN, EDINBURGH

For hundreds of years, the wealthy and powerful of Edinburgh society had lived alongside the poorer classes in high tenement buildings. So lofty and cramped together were the buildings that they hid the sunlight in the street, neighbours could almost shake hands with those living in the structures facing them. The bodily waste of rich and poor alike would fly out the windows and land in the street with an inclusive splat. With the new building work going on to the north, the days of sharing the same filth and disease were ending; now the rich had an escape route. Moving to the New Town must have seemed like journeying to another planet.

Nonetheless, the cry of the Old Town could still be heard, like the song of the sirens, drawing men with money looking for entertainment. Gratifications like the heaving smoky tavern, the city's brothels, the frenzied betting on dog or cockfighting or watching bare-knuckled boxers beating each other to a pulp, could not be found in the New Town.

OLD TOWN, EDINBURGH, FROM THE SCOTT MONUMENT

The abandoned inhabitants of the old city watching those pleasure-seekers walk across the bridges looking forward to an evening's entertainment seethed with resentment. Edinburgh gangs used the thrills within their patches to set traps, knowing the rich would be drawn to the Old Town like moths to a light. These gangs had a violent welcome waiting.

On Hogmanay 1811 (the night of 31 December 1811 and 1 January 1812), those Edinburgh street gangs – known in the city as 'Thief Gangs' – based in Niddry Street, the Canongate, Calton and the Grassmarket, joined together to attack and rob those out enjoying the turn of the year. At sunrise on New Year's Day, many 'gentlemen' lay in the hospital, battered and bruised. They were picked up from the street after lying prostrate amongst the shattered glass from seventy streetlamps, smashed during the turmoil of violence and destruction. Two of the men lay clinging on to life, and both would die in the next few days. One of them was Police Watchman Dugald Campbell, the other a clerk, James Campbell. Dugald was the first police officer to die while on duty in Scotland.

Young apprentice boys would often meet at the bottom of Niddry Street after work at around 9pm. They would pick quarrels with people and often lash out using fists and kicks. Sometimes they would crowd around a passer-by as they walked along the street. A blow of a whistle or a predefined word or phrase would be cried out – this was the signal to attack and rob this unsuspecting victim.

In the days before the New Year celebrations of 1812, these gangs had met up. The youths planned to work together and had decided to give the police a licking. These young ruffians were anxious to get their hands on a police officer called Murray, whom they despised as he often chased them off the North and South Bridges. The gangs had armed themselves with sticks cut from trees in the city's Meadows.

At 11pm on 31 December 1811, the gangs took to the streets. The affluent were attacked and robbed, often beaten during the assaults. The police turned out in large numbers and tried to keep order in the busy, bustling streets. They managed to drive the gangs out of Hunter Square and off the South Bridge. On the Royal Mile, gang members chased a police officer up the road – he was tripped as he ran and fell to the ground. The gang set about him, hitting him over and over with sticks. A cry of '*It is the Royal Arch!*' seemed to intensify the beating the man received. Royal Arch was the nickname the gangs had given to Dugald Campbell, who was despised by the young hoodlums. A few people tried to step in and protect the police officer, but they were driven back by the gang members. By the time the gang left to search for new victims, Campbell was lying motionless in the entrance to Stamp Office Close (today Old Stamp Office Close) in a pool of his own blood. He was lifted and taken to the nearby police office, but he was unable to talk and died three days later.

STAMP OFFICE CLOSE, EDINBURGH

In the days and weeks after the events, the shaken authorities rounded up those they believed to be involved in this unrest. Three men were arrested in connection to the murder of the police officer: Hugh MacDonald, Neil Sutherland and Hugh MacIntosh. Sutherland and MacIntosh had fled to Glasgow where they were picked up and taken back to Edinburgh.

All three were tried at the High Court in Edinburgh on 20 March 1812. The charges were:

1. *The murder of Dugald Campbell, police watchman, at the head of Stamp Office Close.*

2. *Knocking down Ensign Humphry Cochrane, of the Renfrew Militia, on the High Street, and robbing him of a silver watch, a watch chain of gold, two guineas and two one-pound notes, five shillings in silver, a neck handkerchief and a silk pocket handkerchief.*

3. *Knocking down Mr Roger Hog Lawrie, a writer's clerk, on the North Bridge, and robbing him of a seal set in gold, part of a watch chain of gold, a gold watch key and five shillings in silver.*

4. *Knocking down Gustavus Richard Alexander Brown, Esq, on the North Bridge, and robbing him of four pounds sterling in notes, ten shillings in silver, a penknife and a round hat.*

5. *Knocking down Mr Francis James Hughes, near the Tron Church, and robbing him of a gold repeating watch, a gold watch chain, four seals set in gold, a gold watch key and a round hat.*

6. *Assaulting Mr Nicol Allan, Manager of the Hercules Insurance Company, near the Tron Church, and robbing him of a yellow metal hunting watch, a gold watch chain, two seals set in gold, a gold watch key, and 14 shillings in silver.*

7. *Knocking down Mr Duncan Ferguson, writer, near Barclay's Tavern, Adam Square, and robbing him of a gold seal, a gold watch chain, a round hat and nine shillings in silver.*

8. *Assaulting Mr David Scott Kinloch MacLaurin, on the South Bridge, and robbing him of two gold watch cases, a pocket-handkerchief, a round hat and six shillings in silver.*

9. *Knocking down Mr John Buchan Brodie, writer, on the North Bridge, and robbing him of a watch with a shagreen case, a watch ribbon, four seals set in gold, a gold watch key, a blue Morocco leather purse containing a Bank of Scotland one-pound note, a seven-shilling gold piece, eight shillings in silver and a round hat.*

10. *Assaulting Mr Duncan MacLauchlan, student of medicine, on the South Bridge, and robbing him of a round hat, a pocket-handkerchief and a pair of gloves.*

11. *Knocking down Mr Peter Bruce, student of medicine, on the South Bridge, and robbing him of a green silk purse, five shillings and sixpence in silver, a gold ring and a round hat.*

All three pled not guilty.

Many witnesses were brought out by the prosecution, the first, an apprentice blockmaker, John Thompson. He told of seeing a mob chase a gentleman into Assembly Close where he was knocked down. He then spoke of seeing Campbell attacked by a mob at Stamp Office Close. He witnessed the police officer being struck after falling. Thomson said that he ran to Campbell's assistance but was hit on the hand by a gang member who was wielding a stick. The witness stated that as the attack took place, he heard a member of the mob say, '*Take his life*'; and at the same time, a cry of '*Mind the Royal Arch*', which he took as an attempt to save the police officer. He told the court that the gang was notified about a further disturbance that was taking place around the Tron Church. They all left the police officer and ran off towards the Tron. The witness, along with another man, helped the wounded officer to his feet and took him to the nearest police office. Thompson said that Campbell was not talking but was groaning a great deal.

Sergeant James Walker affirmed that when Campbell arrived at the office, he was perfectly incapable of giving any account of what happened. He was left with Mr D Gray, who lived at the police office.

EDINBURGH CASTLE, FROM THE GRASSMARKET

EDINBURGH CASTLE

Gray called a doctor and Campbell was taken to the Royal Infirmary where he died on 3 January 1812.

Another witness called to give evidence was Ensign Humphrey Cochrane, a soldier serving in the Renfrewshire Militia, who was stationed at Edinburgh Castle. He told the court that while walking up the High Street towards the castle, he was attacked and dragged into a close where he was beaten and robbed. Cochrane added that he was knocked down while running away from the disturbances and that while he was being attacked his assailants never asked if he had any money. They just roughly took his cash from his person. He stated that there was a great mob but could not identify any of the accused.

Roger Hog Lawrie told of being on the North Bridge just before midnight despite being forewarned by a young boy that gentlemen were being attacked and robbed. A handful of young men surrounded him and asked him for money for drink and he gave them a crown. He was then knocked to the ground but got up again at once. As he was making his way away from the trouble, he was blocked by a man wearing a grey jacket and carrying a stick. The stranger raised his arm as if to strike Lawrie. The attacker paused and grabbed the cowering man's watch, but the chain broke. The thief got away with part of the chain and a seal. Lawrie also handed over money for fear of being beaten with the staff. He was shown a stick in court and thought it was the one that was used against him by the man in the grey jacket.

Francis James Hughes stated that he was walking between the North and South Bridges at about midnight when he was attacked by a party of young men. He recounted that as they passed, he heard a word that was a signal for the attack. He was knocked down and robbed but got up and approached the man who had his possessions, only to be assaulted once more.

Nicol Allan, a manager at the Hercules Insurance Company, said that he was on the streets at around 1am. He was knocked down by a blow to his forehead. Allan got up and walked on. He was attacked again but managed to hit the man who had assaulted him with his walking cane before being knocked down once more. He was then robbed while he lay on the ground. Stunned and dishevelled, Allan got to his feet and tried to get away from the trouble. Allan fled, only to be attacked and mugged again by a different gang. Battered and bruised, the unfortunate man made his way to the police office on the Royal Mile.

Duncan Fergusson, a clerk, said that on the night in question he was drinking in Barclay's Tavern in Adam Square. (The pub no longer exists but was located somewhere between the George IV Bridge and the South Bridge.) Fergusson left at about midnight. When he and a companion reached the South Bridge, they were attacked. Fergusson was knocked down but did not realise that he had been robbed; it was only after returning to the tavern that someone pointed out his watch was missing. Fergusson noticed that along with the watch, his seal and money had also been taken.

The next witness was John Brodie, who stated that at 12.30am he was passing Milne's Square at which point he saw young men carrying large bludgeons. Brodie told the court that he initially thought that the armed men had been fighting each other. Suddenly one of the men struck him a violent blow. During the attack, Brodie called for the police, but the attacker sneered, 'Your police is long gone'.

Brodie was struck again and fell unconscious. When he came round, he could feel two sets of hands rifling through his pockets. A third person ripped his watch from him, and a little boy took his hat. When asked if he could identify any of his attackers, he looked at the dock and stated that Neil Sutherland could be the one who struck the first blow.

Medical student, Duncan MacLauchlan, was the next person called to give evidence. Duncan stated that on the night in question, a group of young boys told him and his friend Mr Bruce not to go forward or they would be murdered. The pair ignored the advice and were attacked and robbed. Duncan was more assured than the previous witness that Neil Sutherland had been one of his attackers.

John Thompson told the court that as he was going up the High

Street about 11pm on 31 December, he met Dugald Campbell near The Cross. *The* witness told the police officer not to go down the street as he would be attacked, to which Campbell replied, '*Damn the fear!*' before walking towards the Tron Church. Thompson stated that he then saw a mob attack the police officer at Stamp Office Close. As the ferocious attack took place, Thompson said he heard the name *Boatswain* used, which he understood to be the nickname given to Hugh MacDonald. As the blows rained down on the police officer, he heard someone shout, '*Marr him*', which he did not understand, but it may have been short or street talk for murder him. Thompson also heard Campbell cry, '*Murder*'. He said that all the accused were there, and all were carrying sticks. He stated that MacDonald was dressed in a greatcoat although he usually wore a jacket. He also stated that as the Moon was bright and shining on the north side of the High Street, he could see all the accused clearly and he knew them all by sight, especially MacIntosh who worked in Blair Street.

EDINBURGH HIGH STREET

Another witness to the deadly attack on Dugald Campbell was a sailor, John Black. He testified that he saw the mob chase Campbell up the street. As the police officer tried to escape, a man called

Johnstone tripped up the fleeing constable and hit him as he fell. He also saw the man named Boatswain kick the officer. Black stated that he witnessed Sutherland at the scene but did not see him engage in any acts of violence. The witness told of seeing MacIntosh strike the police officer with a stick. Black asserted that he had gone to assist the police officer but was driven back, receiving a blow to the wrist.

CANONGATE JAIL, THE TOLLBOOTH, EDINBURGH

John Gilchrist was another who saw the police officer being attacked. He told the court that he was near the Tron Church and saw a group of lads and boys with sticks. He then heard a cry of, *'There is a policeman'*, and saw the crowd run after the officer. Gilchrist later saw Campbell lying on the ground with a group around him striking and kicking him. He stated that he did not see any of the prisoners in the dock engage in violence against the officer. Although Gilchrist identified MacDonald and MacIntosh as being at the scene he did not see Sutherland. Gilchrist also heard the name Boatswain, and one of the lads shout, *'It is the Royal Arch!'*, which he took to be the nickname given to the police officer being attacked.

14

Some of the gang members who were held in custody were brought out to assist the prosecution. John Tasker was held in the Canongate Jail. He stated that he knew several of the youths who would meet at the bottom of Niddry Street when they finished work at about 9pm. Tasker added that they met about three times a week and called themselves the *Keellies*. He had been part of this gang for about six months. The former gang member told the court that the purpose of the meeting was to pick fights with people. Tasker stated that he did not see anyone being robbed or the gang committing robberies but admitted he had heard it had happened. Tasker admitted that he knew a share in whisky given to him had been obtained illegally. The witness confessed to having also heard of stolen cheese having been shared out to gang members.

EDINBURGH NEW TOWN

Tasker added that three or four weeks before the New Year the gangs had a plan to battle with the police on Hogmanay. Murray, a police officer, was to be hunted down and singled out, as the groups thought him a wicked man, who chased them off the bridge. One of the accused, MacIntosh, told the witness to go to the Meadows and cut sticks so they would be well-armed to give the police a licking. He stated that the Niddry Street gang were planning to join other street gangs from the Canongate, Calton and Grassmarket. He said that the groups were also planning to attack and rob the better off. The well-to-do would come across from the New Town to see in the New Year in the heaving, rowdy and raucous taverns of the Old Town. He stated that Sutherland had indicated that he hoped to get a new hat during one of the robberies. Tasker also claimed that MacIntosh being a fifer (flute player) in the local militia corps, made a bugle that had a particular whistle. A blow on that bugle was used as a signal and he also stated that the other gangs had whistles that they used for the same purpose.

Another gang member, John Kidd, a prisoner in the Tolbooth was brought out as a witness. Kidd had heard of a plan to give the police a licking on New Year's morning and to steal hats from the affluent who ventured into the Old Town. Kidd stated the reason for attacking the police was to drive them from the streets so the gangs could target the gentlemen who were out celebrating the turn of the year. He stated that on the night in question he saw a few 'gentlemen' attacked but added that no tradesmen were molested.

William Swan, a prisoner in Edinburgh Jail, spoke of meeting Sutherland and MacIntosh on the South Bridge before the New Year and being told that they would give the police a killing. He was also informed that the Niddry Street gang was to be joined by the Canongate lads. He told the court of witnessing riots in Edinburgh on the last night of 1811.

With all these witnesses for the prosecution, things were not looking good for the three accused. However, witnesses did come forward for their defence. Margaret Ross, a thirteen-year-old girl, said that she saw MacDonald at home on the night in question between 9pm and 10pm. Although he was drunk, he remained indoors until after midnight. Two of MacIntosh's work colleagues, George Petrie and John Riddel, both shoemakers, stated that on

Hogmanay night the accused worked late: till near 12am. Janet Ross, who was the sister of Margaret, lived in Blair Street. She said that she had known MacDonald for a long time and that she thought him a good character, mild and obliging. Shoemaker James Cameron thought MacDonald a sober, innocent, regular man, and he went on to say that he had confidence in him as honest and faithful. James Anderson who had employed MacDonald for four months stated that MacDonald was sober, honest and respectable. Joseph Petrie described Sutherland as a quiet youth.

SOUTH BRDGE AND COWGATE, EDINBURGH

The jury retired at 4am on 21 March and nine hours later the judge was told a verdict had been agreed. A guard of the Edinburgh Volunteers was stationed in and around the court to keep the peace. The jury unanimously found Hugh MacIntosh guilty of murder and

Hugh MacDonald and Neil Sutherland guilty of robbery. All three prisoners were sentenced to death. It was stated that the execution of the condemned men was to be held across the road from the Stamp Office Close, opposite the spot where the police officer had been attacked. The date of the execution was to be 22 April. After his death, the body of Hugh MacIntosh was to be handed over to the surgeons to be dissected.

On the day of their execution, the three men were up early, their iron shackles were removed, and they had breakfast. The prison chaplain spent time in prayer with the condemned men. They were offered wine and water by Mr Sibbald, the 'Captain' of the prison, which at first, they all refused. After encouragement, they sipped the wine; the rest was given to the guards. The men declined the offer of a coach to the place of execution preferring to walk instead.

EDINBURGH HIGH STREET

The last day of their lives was sunny and warm as they made their way through the crowds. The authorities were expecting trouble from the assembled masses. To keep order, four hundred men of the

Royal Perthshire Militia were lining the High Street and two hundred Royal Edinburgh Volunteers were stationed in Hunter Square. A reserve force (the 6th Dragoons) was posted in Nicolson Street.

While they were on the run and hiding out in Glasgow, MacIntosh and Sutherland had professed that there was no God and afterlife. Understandably, they seemed to have reconsidered. Both were getting comfort from the presence of the clergy on the scaffold. At precisely 3.30pm, Hugh MacIntosh (aged sixteen), Hugh MacDonald and Neil Sutherland (both aged eighteen) were hanged.

II
Police Watchmen Robert Simpson and Henry Pearson
Greenock Burgh Police

---

31 January 1820

On the evening of Saturday, 31 July 1820, a group of soldiers serving in the 13th Regiment of Foot were drinking heavily in a house in Shannon's Close in the port town of Greenock (the close was in the vicinity of what is now East Shaw Street, near the harbour). Two of the soldiers who had ventured outside spotted a sailor by the name of McIntosh, who stayed in the lodging house next door. The two drunk soldiers immediately began to insult him. Not wanting any trouble, the sailor walked with them into their lodging, offering to get them a dram. The sailor, knowing perhaps that there had already been trouble between the two military factions, decided not to drink with the soldiers. Instead, he turned and walked out of the house. As he left, another three soldiers who were standing by the door attacked him. He was knocked to the ground and beaten unconscious. A group of women who witnessed the attack carried him to his house.

The drunk soldiers continued to cause a disturbance by trying to pick fights with passers-by. Soon another seafarer, Robert Robertson, who was returning from visiting a friend was accosted in the street and challenged to fight. The sailor stated that he had no wish for trouble and advised them to return to their house. Robertson was grabbed and dragged into a nearby tavern in Shannon's Close that stood directly below the soldier's lodgings. The military men beat the sailor with a candlestick and would have killed him if the battered and bruised sailor had not been dragged away by the landlord and landlady. The stunned and semi-conscious sailor crawled under a bed to escape the beating.

A large crowd, alerted by the landlady's screams, had gathered outside the pub and were trying to break down the front door. Stones were hurled through the window as news of the assault going on inside the building spread. The property owner, Alexander Cochrane, escaped out a back window and ran to fetch the guard. Among the crowd outside the tavern was a river pilot, John MacCorquindale, who was also a special constable. He demanded admittance to the premises. While the crowd outside besieged the inn, the soldiers went upstairs and grabbed muskets. One of them fired a shot out the window. A young sailor, Archibald Morrison, who was standing at the head of the close watching the events taking place and not involved in the disorder, was hit in the stomach.

The sound of the gunfire caused the crowd to flee, screaming in a state of panic. Harbour Police Watchman Robert Simpson walked up the close with his hands aloft, pleading with the soldiers to cease firing. He promised that if the troops put down their guns and came from the building they would not be *molested*. He also explained that like them, he had also served the King, on board a man-o'-war. He was told that if he came any farther, he would be shot. Suddenly another shot split the air and Simpson fell. A young woman, Flora Muir, called to the soldier at the window to stop firing till she took in the body. A soldier at the window called out to Flora that he would fire on anyone who approached the wounded man. She retreated but again shouted at the soldier to let her assist Simpson. This time the man at the window called out, *'Drag him in then, and be damned to you'*. It is not clear if the soldier was giving permission to approach Simpson or if yet again it was a warning. Another woman who was in the close, Mary Taylor, tried to lift Simpson but was unable to do so.

Another member of the Harbour Police, Henry Pearson, upon seeing his colleague hit and fall to the ground, called out, '*Will no one go forward and assist poor Robert Simpson?*' Bravely, he made his way along to try and reach his fellow officer. A shot followed by others brought Pearson down. He was severely wounded and would die from his injuries two hours later. Shortly after Pearson was hit, soldiers appeared on the scene and the troops in the building were ordered by a sergeant to surrender. They refused until a senior officer appeared with reinforcements. It was only then that the soldiers left the lodging house. They were placed under arrest and marched through a sizeable sullen crowd that had gathered on the streets of Greenock.

Alexander Morrison, the first person shot by the soldiers, died from his wounds the next day. Robert Robertson, the sailor who had been the catalyst for the night's tragic events, was found under a bed, savagely beaten. The Master of Police who found Robertson described him in the press as in a miserable state.

On Tuesday, 7 November 1820, Robert Surrage, John Dempsey, John Beck, Joseph Elliot, Malachi Clinton and Patrick Lynch (all privates in the 13th Regiment of Foot) were tried at the High Court in Edinburgh for murder.

Most witnesses claimed to have seen shots being fired from the window of the building in Shannon's Close but could not make out who was firing. Alexander Cochrane, the innkeeper who had escaped out of the window of the tavern to fetch help when the sailor Robertson was attacked, told the court that Dempsey had threatened to blow his brains out for rushing off and getting the guard. One of the guards, Sergeant MacLurg, stated that when he arrived at Shannon's Close, Surrage shouted from the window, '*Who goes there?*' MacLurg replied, '*The sergeant of the guard*'. When told to fall back, MacLurg shouted, '*Don't fire, tis the guard, this is a bad night's work*'. The sergeant said that Dempsey presented his musket at him and cocked it. The gun was knocked aside by a soldier called Colwell as it went off.

After all the evidence was heard, the Lord Advocate addressed the jury and he told them that there was not sufficient proof against Privates Elliot, Beck and Lynch, but asked for a guilty verdict against Surrage and Dempsey. The jury returned and, taking the Lord Advocate's advice, returned a verdict of not guilty on Beck, not proven for Elliot and Lynch and guilty on Surrage and Dempsey. They also recommended mercy be shown to Surrage. The judge sentenced both men to death. Surrage sobbed as he sat in the dock. The judge ordered that after their execution, the bodies were to be given to Dr Munro for dissection.

Robert Surrage had his sentence mitigated to transportation for life. The wintry weather kept the crowds down on the freezing morning of Wednesday, 13 December 1820. John Dempsey was led to the scaffold on Edinburgh's High Street. He was followed up the steps by his priest, Father Wallace. Dempsey bowed respectfully at the watching city magistrates and shook hands with those around him. The hangman placed a noose around his neck while he continued to pray, before declaring loudly, '*I am innocent of the charge against me*'. The condemned man gave the hangman the signal that he was ready to meet his maker. The executioner pulled the lever and Dempsey fell to his death. His body was left to swing before being cut down and taken to Edinburgh's Royal College of Surgeons for dissection.

III
Special Constable Alexander Ross
Girvan Burgh Police

12 July 1831

Scotland at the turn of the eighteenth and during the early nineteenth century was a volatile land. The poor were desperate for electoral reform and better working conditions, with representation in Parliament and the workplace high on the agenda. Mass meetings and marches were held in towns and cities throughout the country. At one such meeting in Girvan, the reformers were interrupted by a large party of Orangemen, by nature loyal to the Crown and establishment. (They get their name from William Prince of Orange, whose Protestant army, supported politically by the Catholic Papal States, defeated and forced into exile the Catholic Stuart King James VII of Scotland and II of England at the Battle of the Boyne in Ireland in 1690.) A fight broke out between the two parties. This confrontation forged bitter resentment between the townspeople and those in the local Orange Lodge.

The twelfth of July is the highlight of the traditional marching month for the Orange Order. When members of the Girvan Orange Lodge invited outlying lodges to march into Girvan on 12 July 1831, the townspeople, many of them Catholics of Irish origin, were determined to stop them. The town's magistrates asked the Sheriff of Ayr that a force be sent to Girvan to keep the peace. The Sheriff arrived in Girvan with one hundred police batons and a request to raise a force of special constables from amongst the population to protect the town. The people of Girvan refused to sign up unless the Orangemen were denied entry into the town officially. The Sheriff and magistrates visited the local Orange Lodges and persuaded them not to march into Girvan town centre but bypass it and head straight to a meeting place south of the town.

Early on the morning of 12 July, a large body of Orangemen turned up on the outskirts of the town. They were determined to march into Girvan. When asked, some agreed to divert their march so they would not enter the town centre but many of them refused, resolved on entering the town. Their route, now the B734, was blocked by a large body of constables; 150 of them had been sworn in that morning. The townspeople lined the fields on either side of the road. As tempers flared, stones were thrown by locals at the side of the road into the ranks of the Orangemen. One Orangeman stepped from the fifth or sixth rank and levelled a gun, pointing it down the road in the direction of the police constables, and fired. A shot rang out, a wisp of white smoke drifted into the air, and police officer Alexander Ross fell to the ground clutching his belly. He cried, '*Oh, I am shot!*' and died where he lay. Another police officer, Alexander

Stevens, tried to grab the gun from the man who fired, and as the two men grappled, the constable was struck on the back of the head from behind by a sword or club and was left lying senseless.

More shots rang out as the marchers fired. Screaming women and children in a blind panic fled for their lives, escaping in all directions. A running battle broke out as the Orangemen armed with guns, pistols, swords, pikes and bayonets attacked both the civilians and the police. The panic-stricken crowd fled by road in the direction of the town; others ran through the fields. The Water of Girvan prevented those to the north from escaping. A few waded into the water and tried to swim to safety. Stones and rocks fell on one blood-soaked constable as he swam across the river.

The Orangemen now marched, heading into the town, firing their guns and pistols. They were attacking all those who stood in their way and smashing windows en route rampaging and shouting at the tops of their voices, *'This town is our own'*. They made their way along Montgomerie Street, down past the public buildings and on to Doune Park. The marchers advanced through the town, savagely assaulting everyone they came upon. One older man, Gilbert Davidson, who was on his way to weed his fields was slashed on the head and shoulders and left lying at the side of the road. A weaver, David McQueen, lost the sight of one eye after being attacked.

A police officer by the name of Orr was attacked opposite the Town Hall, one of several officers severely beaten. He was knocked down and slashed with swords, punched and kicked as he lay defenceless. One Orangemen held a pistol to Orr's face and fired. The bullet grazed the officer's head.

At the day's end when the Orangemen had left Girvan, Constable Alexander Ross lay dead, four men were in a dangerous condition and eight were severely injured. More were bruised and bleeding. Multiple buildings were damaged and pockmarked by gunfire, including the house of the town's Baillie.

The authorities acted quickly and arrested thirty-one men within forty-eight hours. One of the men in custody was Samuel Waugh, the man thought to have been responsible for the fatal shooting. The police apprehended Waugh in Newton Stewart. The trial of the thirty-one accused was initially to take place in the town of Ayr. As Ayr was in the vicinity of the crime, making it hard to obtain an impartial jury, at the behest of the defence, the trial was moved to Edinburgh. There, at the High Court on 29 December 1831, Samuel Waugh and John Ramsey stood in the dock. Ramsey was accused of leading the Orangemen on the day of the death of the police officer and ordering them to open fire.

ALEXANDER ROSS MARKER
(Gary Knight)

Those Orangemen acting as witnesses stated that Ramsey, who kept a public house in Maybole, organised the marchers on the road outside Girvan. Ramsey, according to the witnesses, ordered those carrying arms to the front of the procession. One of the men, John Coffin, a shoemaker from Ayr, a drummer to the lodge in Crosshill, Ayrshire, stated that the only armed men he saw were two with fowling guns who were protecting his lodge's colours. Coffin denied seeing anyone else carrying arms. The witness also told the court that he distinctly heard John Ramsey say to the ranks of marchers that no one was to molest any person unless attacked. All the Orangemen told of having stones thrown at them by a crowd of people from the town.

Gilbert Gray, sworn in as a special constable on the day of the shooting, told the court that Ramsey came up to speak to the constables. Gray stated, that at the time, stones were raining down on them, thrown mostly by boys. Gray also said there was one – or two men – chucking missiles at the Orangemen, who threw objects back. He then told of seeing Waugh fire a shot, and the ball hitting Constable Ross.

Another special constable, James MacLure, seemed to contradict the other witnesses. He stated it was the Orangemen who started throwing stones at the police. It was only then that the people of Girvan retaliated by lobbing projectiles into the mass of marchers. Gray also claimed that a rock hit a man behind Ramsey, and this led to Ramsey shouting '*Fire!*'. It was at that moment someone fired a shot at the police. James Farrell, a weaver from Maybole and one of the Orangemen, stated that a shout to fire was given by more than two or three people. Farrell also told of being given a pistol as he was an old soldier. He saw Waugh with a gun and observed the accused load it with round ball.

The next witness, Henry MacKeatings, was one of the Girvan townspeople lining the road. MacKeatings said he saw a man he thought to be Waugh step out from the ranks and shoot Ross. MacKeatings admitted that after the shot he picked up a stone and threw it at Waugh. The rock hit the accused which broke his jaw. He saw Waugh stagger and put his hand to his face. Several townspeople stated that they saw and heard Ramsey give the order to fire.

James Campbell stated that he was yards from Ross. He explained that Ross said to a man he could not identify, '*If you fire that gun, I will apprehend you*'. Campbell noted that the shooter drew back one foot, lifted his gun to his shoulder, and fired at Ross. Another man, Alexander McBroom, collaborated this account.

The next witnesses brought out were members of the Orange Lodge. Simon Menoch, a member of the Girvan Lodge, specified that their 12 July march alternated between Girvan and its neighbouring villages. The year before was in Maybole and he told of going to see the Baillie of Girvan, Mr Hunter, after hearing that the Baillie planned to stop the march. Menoch revealed that the Baillie acknowledged that preventing the march would be against the law. The Orangeman also noted that it was common for members on parade to carry arms. John Andrew, Deputy Master of the Girvan Lodge, backed Menoch's statement.

Deputy Grand Master of the Maybole Lodge, Joseph Milliken, stated that he was standing by Ramsey who was not carrying any firearm. Milliken explained that the Orangemen were asked not to enter the town by their planned route but to take an alternative road. Milliken stated that the Orangemen agreed to take the other road, but a body of police officers blocked this way. There was a murmur along the line of constables and insults were shouted out by the police.

A couple of witnesses testified that the Orangemen were fired upon by the Girvan crowd before they fired back. As you might expect, due to the confusion, entrenched views and length of time between the event and the trial, there was a great deal of conflicting evidence given.

The Solicitor General addressed the jury for the Crown. He stated that a guilty of murder verdict for Samuel Waugh was the only reasonable outcome, as it was as clear as if he had pulled a pistol from his pocket and shot his friend on the opposite side of the table. As to Ramsey, he was guilty of being Waugh's instigator and encourager and therefore should be found guilty of culpable homicide.

Thomas Maitland for the defence stated that the Orange march was legal. It was the people of Girvan trying to prevent the parade who were the ones breaking the law. He also argued it could be that on firing their guns when assaulted by missiles, the Orangemen were only defending themselves. If Waugh did fire the fatal shot (and even that was doubtful owing to the confusion), then he was only protecting himself and a charge of culpable homicide would be the right verdict. As for Ramsey, Maitland offered that there was not enough evidence to convict, and the right outcome would be that it was not proven.

The jury retired for a brief time and returned with a verdict of guilty for Samuel Waugh, and not proven for John Ramsey. Waugh was unmoved as the judge sentenced him to be hanged at Ayr. After the execution, the surgeons were to be given the corpse for dissection. The court detained John Ramsey on a charge of mobbing and rioting.

GRAVE OF ALEXANDER ROSS

Taken to Ayr under escort by a party of the Ayrshire Yeomanry and placed in the town jail, Samuel Waugh waited for his execution. While incarcerated and awaiting his fate, he stated that he had not intended to kill Ross. He was not to blame for the police officer's death: his own blood and the blood of Alexander Ross lay upon the people of Girvan. Waugh received a visit from his wife about which the *Perthshire Courier* of 26 January 1832 noted that his wife brought news that she had lost her only child.

On 19 January, five thousand people filled the streets of Ayr. A large body of constables armed with batons and a detachment of the Ayr Yeomanry were in attendance. Brought from the jail just before 2pm, the prisoner was described as thin and middle-aged. He stood on the scaffold facing the crowd along with the Sheriff, Provost and Baillies of Ayr. Executioner Thomas Williams hanged Waugh at 2pm and his body was taken to Edinburgh for handing over to the surgeons.

IV
Police Constable William Ford
Edinburgh City Police

22 April 1840

On St Patrick's Day, 17 March 1840, a large group of men in Edinburgh made their way to King's Park (newspaper reports detailed the incident as taking place at St Ann's Yard which was a little to the northeast of Holyrood Palace). The men were celebrating, and drink was flowing. While watching a hotly contested game of football, a quarrel broke out and soon punches were flying. The scuffle intensified into a wholesale brawl with sticks, bottles and knives; stones and rocks flew. The few police officers on the scene tried to intervene but as soon as they got involved, the brawlers turned on them. Sergeant John Kelly and Constable William Ford received a savage beating; Kelly lay in a dangerous state for days and Ford lingered for more than a month before dying from his injuries.

John McGoveran, John Jones and Thomas McKenna were tried at the High Court in Edinburgh on 22 June 1840, but a lack of evidence and witnesses saw the case dismissed.

V
Town Officer Thomas Corstorphin
Burntisland Burgh Police

19 January 1844

Henderson Sliman was a respectable citizen of Burntisland, Fife. He had been a sailor and later worked for the coastguard in Berwick. In 1844, he should have been enjoying his retirement in his hometown of Burntisland, but the old man was worried about his son Adam. The younger Sliman was showing signs of extreme mental illness, the result of an accident Adam had had while working on a steamer sailing between Berwick and Newcastle. While working on the ship, Adam had suffered a severe blow to the head when struck by a winch. Things got so bad that during the family's return journey to Fife, Adam had to be placed in a straitjacket.

Back at Burntisland things did not improve. Adam was unable to work and relied on the charity of his father. He became convinced that a considerable sum of money had been left to him by a deceased relative. He thought that the cash was being kept from him by the businesspeople of Burntisland and he also believed that his enemies had a large telescope and were watching his every move and that they could tell what he was thinking. It was clear that Adam was an extremely sick man. He issued threats about what would happen if this fictitious money was not returned. Adam was at one time a shoemaker and was in the habit of carrying a shoemaker's knife. He would continuously sharpen it and place it in a leather sheath. His father worried that his son was capable of violence against his perceived enemies and would follow him around the streets.

SHOEMAKER'S KNIFE

The only calming influence on Adam seemed to be his wife and children. Adam never made them feel in any danger, he was a good husband to his wife and father to his four children. But Adam's threatening behaviour became so bad that his father went to see the local magistrate. It was decided to issue a warrant to apprehend the troubled man. This was for his own safety as much as for the protection of the people he was threatening.

On 18 January 1844, two police officers along with Thomas Davie, the Procurator Fiscal for the town, went to Adam's home. One of the constables, William Reekie, was also a porter. When they gained admission to the house, he told Adam that they had brought a parcel for him that had arrived from Edinburgh. Adam, who was sitting at the fire with his youngest child, a five-month-old baby on his knee, realised something was wrong. He sprang up and pulled out his knife, shouting that he would stab the first man that approached him through the heart. The officials, fearing for the child's safety, could only retire from the house.

It became apparent that Adam must be captured as soon as possible as it was discovered that after the failed attempt to take him, he had gone out into the streets of Burntisland with his knife looking for the police constables. A plan was hatched to capture Adam the next day at a spot where no one else would be in danger. The police decided on The Links, on the east side of the town as it was known Adam liked to walk there every day. Another three constables were brought in to help in the arrest. The officers split up so they could approach Adam from more than one direction.

Officer Thomas Corstorphin and another police officer took the higher road while Thomas Davie and two other officers made their way to The Links from the High Street direction. Davie received information that the wanted man was engaged in breaking stones behind Lochie House. Vast quantities of crushed rock were needed for a new road being built. When the three officers approached, Constable Dailly shouted out, '*Adam, go no further, for you are our prisoner!*'

THE LINKS, BURNTISLAND

Adam asked if they had a warrant and although told that they did, he threatened to stab the first man that came for him. As he shouted the warning at the officers, he pulled out his knife. Davie kept Adam at bay with his baton and another officer used a broken wooden fence paling to defend himself. Adam saw the other police officers approaching from the north and turned and made a run for it, taking off through a grass field with the chasing police officers gaining on him.

Adam was now surrounded and using his knife, kept the police at bay. The officers had their batons out. They were taking it in turns to move in to strike the fugitive and at the same time being careful not to come in the way of the thrusts of the knife. Dailly hit Adam on the left arm, then Constable Corstorphin moved in to strike but missed. Adam surged forward and stabbed the officer in the chest. The constable staggered and collapsed onto the ground whereupon he died. Later it would transpire that the stab wound had gone right through the police officer's coat and vest and sliced his heart in two.

Adam made a stabbing motion at Reekie, who swerved the knife thrust and hit Adam over the head with his baton. Adam bolted, running in the direction of the town with the officers in hot pursuit.

He ran up the High Street, bloodied knife in hand, with the chasing officers shouting at the population in the street to keep away from him. Adam reached his own house and barred the entrance. The police, fearing for Adam's wife and children who were in the building alongside him, broke open the kitchen window. Adam's family were removed from the house through the window. By now Adam was standing at the top of the stairs, knife in hand and shouting threats to the police officers who had gained entry through the window in the kitchen. A police officer was placed to the rear of the building in case the wanted man managed to escape. By this time, a large crowd had gathered outside, baying for Adam's blood. The constables at the foot of the stairs had been given pitchforks to defend themselves. The police officers had taken the precaution of bending the points of the forks back, to avoid injuring the deranged man at the top of the steps.

The standoff continued, with no amount of coaxing able to persuade Adam to put down the knife and surrender. A plan was hatched to break through the roof of the house and a slater was called. Gaining entry to the roof, the worker began to strip away the slates. When Adam heard what was going on, he charged down the stairs at the police officers and he barged into one of the constables carrying a pitchfork. The two men fell over a stool and while lying on the floor, Adam was grabbed and held.

Once the siege was over, a feeling of shock spread over the town as both the prisoner and the dead officer were well known. The killer had been born in Burntisland and was a young man of around thirty years. The dead police officer was about ten years older and was from St Andrews. He had been a police officer in Burntisland for about four years and was said to be well respected in the town. His body was sent back to St Andrews. The prisoner was transported to Kirkcaldy Jail and from there to the County Jail at Cupar.

At his trial on 2 February 1844, Adam Sliman was found guilty as libelled. The court decided he was suffering from a state of insanity when the crime was committed. He was to be locked up indefinitely and at the discretion of the Crown.

VI
Police Constable Richard Pace
Edinburghshire Constabulary

1 March 1846

In the mid-1800s, vast works were being conducted on the railways with new lines connecting towns and cities throughout Scotland. This work needed a great deal of labour. Men from Ireland sought employment in the back-breaking and often dangerous work. These men had a reputation of being good workers who liked to drink and play hard. They were in the main good with their fists, as to live in that tough culture you had to be able to stand your ground and fight. Arduous work, heavy drinking and violence was a way of life to the navvies.

Saturday, 28 February 1846, was payday for the navvies working on the Edinburgh to Hawick railway. The drink flowed freely and a group of the workforce drinking in a tavern in Gorebridge, Midlothian, to the south of the capital, were getting drunk and rowdy. A travelling pedlar stopped at the pub. He intended to sell his wares to the railwaymen. The navvies agreed to look at the watches. They refused to hand back the timepieces or pay the money due. The pedlar went to the local police station and informed the constable on duty of the theft of his watches. The police went to the tavern and arrested the two navvies involved; the men were taken and locked up in the station.

When news of this arrest spread to the navvies' camp, between one hundred and fifty and two hundred of them armed themselves with pickaxe handles, sticks, and hedge bills and made their way to Gorebridge. In the early hours of the morning of 1 March 1846, they turned up outside the police station. The mob demanded the return of the two men locked in the cells inside the building. There were only two police officers in the station at the time, a Sergeant Brown and a Constable Christie. The two police officers refused to hand over the prisoners, and the navvies attacked the building. During the fighting, Sergeant Brown received a severe injury after being hit on the head with a pickaxe handle. Soon the mob had forced their way into the station and had smashed down the cell doors. With their liberated compatriots, they set off in the direction of Fushiebridge, about half a mile south-east of Gorebridge.

CONSTABLE PACE KILLED AT GOREBRIDGE

On the way, they met two more police officers, Constable Richard Pace and Railway Policeman John Veitch. The mob immediately set about the officers, beating them savagely. Veitch managed to escape by crawling through a hedge at the side of the road. Now the labourers turned their full attention on the other constable by punching, kicking, stamping and hitting him with clubs, sticks and coshes. When done, they left Constable Pace lying almost dead at the side of the road, around one hundred yards from his front door. Two young lads who had heard the assault found the battered body. Pace never regained consciousness and died soon afterwards.

On Monday morning, outraged Scottish and English navvies armed themselves and they met at Newbattle at 10am, where they were joined by a hundred and fifty miners. With a piper at the front, this force numbering two thousand men marched to the south end of the line at Crichton Muir where the Irishmen were working. The Irish, having heard that a large party of angry men were on their way, fled the scene. The Scots and Englishmen burned down the Irish camp, setting fire to the huts. The local police sent a message to Edinburgh. The authorities, struggling to control order, dispatched a party of Dragoons from Piershill Barracks. By the evening of Monday, 2 March, the military had restored law and order. The police arrested nineteen men involved in the burning of the Irish camp and sent them under escort to Edinburgh.

The situation was still volatile on the morning of Tuesday, 3 March. Around two hundred Irishmen had gathered and intended to march upon Edinburgh. Their purpose was to get at the men locked up for burning the camp. The local Sheriff and a party of the military persuaded them to return to their camp. That Tuesday, the authorities arrested a further nine Scottish navvies.

The local newspapers printed a reward for the men involved in killing the police officer. The information stated that the reward was for £50 and the men wanted were Peter Clark and Patrick Reilly.

Clark was described as:

About 35–40 years of age, 5 feet, 9 in height, stout make, fair complexion, reddish face, sandy-coloured hair, a little curled; small sandy-coloured whiskers, and dressed when last seen, in a bluebonnet, dark-greyish-coloured trousers, drab vest, a green velvet shooting coat, with large navvy boots.

And Reilly as:

About 40 years of age, stout make, 5 feet, 7 in height, dark complexion, black hair, and short black whiskers mixed with a few grey hairs, and dressed when last seen, in a bluebonnet, moleskin jacket, vest and trousers, and large navvy boots.

The report added that since the murder, Reilly had changed his name to his mother's family name of Ryner.

Six men pled guilty to mobbing and rioting and were sentenced at the High Court in Edinburgh on 22 June 1846. They were Patrick Burns, Matthew Clark, George Dunn, Felix Murray, Peter Reilly and Patrick Savage. The judge sentenced each man to transportation for seven years. It seems the two wanted men, Peter Clark and Patrick Reilly, escaped.

The riot and killing of Constable Richard Pace had the effect of stirring up distrust, intolerance and even what we would now call racial hatred for the Irish navvy. It is worth quoting at length the opinion offered by the *Edinburgh Evening Post & Scottish Standard* in its edition of 4 March 1846:

It will be noticed by accounts in our columns of today, that not only have those pests to society, the 'navvies' created a disgraceful riot in our vicinity, but that, melancholy to relate, a constable belonging to the county police has been barbarously murdered. The whole affair is, to the last degree, horrible, and humiliating too – to think that gangs of villains, furnished with abundant employment, in our midst take every occasion of disturbing the peace of our country districts, and committing assaults upon the guardians of the peace. It is quite manifest that the policy which assembles vast bodies of lawless men in our country places, demands a change in our mode of preventive justice. It is absurd and cruel to send out a few unarmed men to cope with hundreds of ruffians, trained amidst Irish vice and ferocity. The county police should, as in Ireland, be armed with both carbines and cutlasses. Had the poor man whose death we have noticed, had such weapons, he might have now been alive; for the navvies like madmen are arrant cowards. . . The punishment should be the whipping-post. The certainty of a flogging would best deter lawless men from crime. What cares a ferocious 'navvie' for twenty days imprisonment? The fellow has lived on potatoes and water in a mud cabin hitherto – he gets better house-room and better food in prison.

There is no excuse for either the killing of this police officer nor the violence that frequently followed men working on the great building projects. Nevertheless, I wonder if the writer of the above article ever gave a thought to the terrible dangers and awful conditions these men had to face day in, day out, as he sat on a train and took a journey on one of the new railway lines.

VII
Police Watchman John Colquhoun
City of Glasgow Police

4 April 1847

The nature of policing takes police officers into dangerous situations often in the dead of night on their own. On 4 April 1847, a passer-by found Police Watchman John Colquhoun lying dead on his beat in Glasgow. A post-mortem conducted on the police officer's body indicated that a blow to the head fracturing his skull had killed the officer. The injury to the police officer seemed to have been caused by a heavy blunt object. The wound was an inch above the ear.

Doctors Buchanan and Easton examined the body, and both agreed that this injury was not accidental. Colquhoun's death remained unsolved. The *Caledonian Mercury* of Monday, 12 April 1847, wrote that Colquhoun was from Edinburgh, had served in the Glasgow Police Force for three years, and had never been reported for a fault.

VIII
Special Constable James Alexander
City of Glasgow Police

8 March 1848

The 1840s were known as 'The Hungry Forties' as a serious of disastrous harvests caused widespread food shortages in Europe. The potato famine had a devastating effect on Ireland and to a lesser extent the Scottish Highlands. Many from the Highlands were forced to leave their home and emigrate, heading either overseas or into the industrial cities of the Central Belt of Scotland looking for work.

Glasgow was struggling to cope with the high number of impoverished and unemployed inhabitants, with payment of food in return for work customary practice. On Monday, 6 March 1848, a mass meeting was held on Glasgow Green, where the unemployed demanded two shillings a day for working. A large section of the crowd left the Green and marched to the nearby police buildings where the magistrates were sitting. The mob demanded food or employment. Instead, the authorities offered tickets for the soup kitchen. The crowd returned to the Green and informed those assembled about the offer of food. One man, George Smith, said that they would not go to the soup kitchen and would not go back to their starving families empty-handed. He stated, *'Let us go, in a body, to the town and have our rights'*.

A loud cheer erupted at this show of defiance. One man stood up and told the crowd that if he had three hundred men, he would go into town and return with enough bread to give everyone a loaf.

The now infuriated crowd left the Green ripping metal railings from a fence on Monteith Row; houses in the Row had their windows broken by the mob. They marched to Canning Street which stretched between Abercromby Street and Bridgeton Cross (now part of London Road). There, they forced their way into and looted the premises of the Calton and Bridgeton Baking Society. The angry mob smashed their way into a nearby grocer's shop and gutted it. A large crowd in the Gallowgate looted shops including a gun shop where they took guns, pistols and powder flasks.

Unemployed men, desperate and angry, reinforced those looting. News of the disturbance spread, and others made their way to claim their share. The mob broke into shops along London Street. The papers described a vast mob, consisting of men and boys, amongst whom were also women of the lower class, proceeding along Argyle Street, smashing windows, and plundering bakers and provision shops of their content. Ransacked gun shops had their deadly contents taken and a cart loaded with meal was stopped in Buchanan Street. The sacks were ripped open and the contents were taken by the throng. The Argyle Arcade, although attacked, shut the gates at both ends, sparing it from destruction. The crowd shooting in the air and crying out, 'Bread or Revolution' and 'Vive la Révolution', marched across the Broomielaw Bridge spanning the River Clyde. On the south side of the river shops suffered looting. In a watchmaker's premises, a shop boy had a gun pointed at his head and received a threat of being shot if he offered any resistance. The vast crowd proceeded along Nicholson Street, Oxford Street and Clyde Street before heading back to the north side of the river, smashing windows as they went. The Saltmarket received widespread damage as disturbances spread to the area.

The city authorities were helpless and could not act quickly. A messenger informed the barracks in Gallowgate Street of the situation. Most soldiers were away on exercise and so the cavalry in Eglinton Street Barracks prepared to march into town, but it took a while for the military to make an appearance. When troops did eventually appear, they arrived with a body of police officers. It looked like a battle might flare up between the authorities and those involved in the unrest. However, on seeing the cavalrymen pull out their rifles, the crowd fled in all directions. Anyone caught fleeing with looted merchandise was apprehended. The police arrested one woman as she rolled a colossal cheese, too big to carry, along the street. Another woman arrested had two large rounds of cheese under each arm and had her apron full of meal which she held with her teeth.

A large force of infantry arrived in the town and crossed the river to the Gorbals, supported by special constables who had recently been sworn in. The Gorbals was to be the scene of rioting and looting. Factories and other works had closed for the evening and this reinforced the crowd in Saltmarket Street. The cavalry repeatedly charged the inflated mob. Baillie Stewart, escorted by cavalry, was moving around the city and when he came upon a large group, he read the Riot Act demanding the crowd disperse.

As the evening progressed, the disturbances died down and surprisingly the casualties were light. One man was injured when a gun fired by a protestor burst near him and a boy had his head slashed by a sabre near Glasgow Cross. A dragoon was hurt when he fell from his startled and frightened horse. That night, the city remained tense; all Glasgow's businesses and theatres remained shut.

Early the next morning, Tuesday, 7 March, the streets of Glasgow were quiet. At around midday, large groups made their way to Glasgow Green. The leaders of the crowd stood up and talked about the tyranny forced upon them. They decided to march to the nearby factories and mills, demanding the people employed in them down tools and stop working. The marchers hoped the workers would join the struggle against the authorities.

The crowd marched to a mill in Bridgeton where they demanded that the workers leave the premises and join the protest. The mob physically dragged the workers out when they refused to join the rioters. The authorities sent a detachment of the Royal Veteran Battalion of Pensioners to protect the mill workers. With protection from the military, work resumed in the mill. Soon the machinery was again in motion and production of goods started once more.

A battle erupted out in the street with the pensioners having missiles rain down on them and many of the soldiers were injured. A senior police officer at the scene, Assistant Superintendent Smart, gave the troops the order to fire on the crowd. The volunteers levelled their muskets and fired into the mob. When the smoke lifted, several lay wounded and one man, Carruth, was dead. James Alexander, a shop owner, and a special constable had been standing outside his shop, desperately trying to persuade the crowd to disperse. He had been shot in the back and died from his injuries. Six more people were to die from their wounds in the next few days.

Military reinforcements marched into the city. These troops included the Third Royal Irish Dragoons who went to Bridgeton, the scene of the fatal shootings. The 1st Royals and the 71st Regiment of Foot marched into the city, and a deployment of special constables arrived from the outlying areas.

With this show of force, things quietened down but the next day, a large crowd appeared on Glasgow Green and this time the cavalry dispersed them. The tension was on a knife-edge, but things remained quiet, policing in the area being helped by a considerable number of workers from the factories and mills sworn in as special constables. The authorities estimated the total damage done in the city to amount to about £12,000.

On the same week, serious disorder broke out in both Edinburgh and London. The authorities were fearful of a public uprising and arrested sixty-four people in Glasgow – twenty were found guilty and convicted. George Smith, transported for mobbing for eighteen years, received the harshest punishment.

IX
Police Constable Ewan McDonald
Dundee City Police

22 June 1851

In the early hours of Sunday, 22 June 1851, a large group of weavers had gathered about one hundred yards east of the junction of Princess Street and Arbroath Road in the East End of Dundee. This area of the city was inhabited by weavers. The crowd of between twenty to thirty men were shouting and arguing after spending a night drinking. This disturbance attracted three police constables: Ewan McDonald, Samuel Aitken and William Wright.

The three police officers approached the crowd and Aitken asked them to quieten down and disperse. The men immediately attacked the officer. He was punched and kicked, and he fell to the ground. A large-scale fight followed as the other two constables, whose batons were drawn, were also attacked and knocked to the floor. The officers got to their feet and were a second time thrown down. This time,

Constable Ewan McDonald cried out, '*Oh Willie, Willie, I am stabbed!*'. When his colleagues tried to lift the stricken officer, the dying man said, '*Willie, I am gone!*'.

Hearing the police officer's cry and realising the seriousness of the situation, and after seeing four ploughmen from the Mains of Fintry along with a fifth man approach, a mechanic, the weavers turned and fled the scene. Constable Wright ran after one man and managed to catch him. He was James MacCulloch, one of the men who took a leading role in attacking the police officers. The injured police officer was carried to a nearby pub, the Atholl Brose. Someone went to fetch the police surgeon, Dr Alex Webster, and to inform Superintendent Mackey as to what had happened. Both hurried to the scene but when they reached the Atholl Brose it was too late. Ewan McDonald had died from his wounds. He was to leave a wife and a young child behind.

Mackey ordered a general search and the setting up of roadblocks. The police searched every house in the area. In the dragnet, James Edgar was discovered lying in bed with a head injury. He told the police that he had fallen down the stairs. On a chair by the bed were a pile of neatly-placed clothes, which showed no signs of being stained with blood. As the man's head wound had bled heavily and had been a recent injury, the police found the absence of bloodstains on the clothes disturbing. The police made their way to the Edgar's sister's house where they found bloodstained clothing steeping in a bowl of water. The police also found a knife in a jug on the mantelpiece. Edgar, also known as James Aiger, was apprehended and taken to the police office.

Later that day, vast crowds of people turned up to look at the site of the fatal stabbing. Blood could still be seen on two walls on either side of the road. On Monday, 23 June, Dr Webster examined the body. He was to report that a stab wound to the left breast had killed the police officer. The knife had travelled through clothing, as well as the third and fourth ribs before penetrating the heart. In the doctor's opinion the wound was inflicted by a small, sharp instrument.

At the High Court in Perth on Wednesday, 15 October 1851, Aiger (as Edgar was referred to in court) and James MacCulloch pled not guilty. Aiger stated that he had been drinking in the Atholl Brose on the night of the police officer's death with eight or nine friends. On leaving the pub, he said he was approached by two police officers who, without any provocation, hit him and knocked him down with their batons. Aiger asserted that he lay on the ground dazed and had no recollection of the resulting dispute. He did admit to carrying a small knife which he used for cutting tobacco. He stated that to his knowledge he did not stab a police officer.

PERTH HIGH COURT
(Perth Museum and Art Gallery)

MacCulloch also stated that he had been drinking in the Atholl Brose. When he and his friends left, a police officer came up and told them to move on. He heard a scuffle and on turning around saw the police knock Aiger down to the ground. MacCulloch also denied stabbing anyone that night. Witnesses described having seen the fight between the weavers and the police, but none of them saw the deadly stab wound inflicted. With this evidence heard, the prosecution withdrew the charge of assault and murder and sought a conviction of assault.

On summoning up, the Lord Justice Clerk confirmed the change to the lesser charge of assault, explaining that the prosecution had failed to prove that either of the prisoners had inflicted the fatal wound. He also stated that the blood on Aiger's clothing could not have come from the officer as it was on the inside of the accused man's jacket. The blood had come from the accused's wounds. Although no one had seen Aiger or MacCulloch stab Constable McDonald, witnesses had seen both men fight with the police on the night in question. The jury returned with a verdict of guilty of assault. Both men were sentenced to eighteen months of hard labour. The judge stated that if the prosecution had proved that either prisoner had used a knife during the fight, and if the evidence was insufficient for a murder charge, the judge would have ordered a sentence of transportation for life.

During the trial, it came out that the three police officers, Ewan McDonald, Samuel Aitken and William Wright had gone into the *Atholl Brose* to have a pint of beer. They stated that they did not realise it was against regulations for a police officer to drink while on duty. The *Dundee, Perth and Cupar Advertiser* of 17 October 1851 declared that the Atholl Brose had been the focus of complaints regarding rowdy behaviour. Shortly after the trial, the publican, Mr Grant, had his licence taken away.

X
Police Constable Charles Angus
Edinburgh City Police

---

6 June 1858

Police Constable Charles Angus was on patrol in Edinburgh's Canongate on the evening of Saturday, 29 May 1858, when he witnessed a disturbance. It appeared as if a drunk had knocked over an apple seller's stand. An argument was taking place and the police officer hurried over to the scene. The man involved in the brawl was Alexander

Smith, a seafarer from Plymouth.* He was not drunk but was suffering from what we today would call serious mental health issues.

POLICE BOX, CANONGATE/CRANSTON STREET, EDINBURGH

Smith thought he was dead. He believed that his wife had poisoned him with mercury sixteen months before. The disturbed man became convinced that he did not have a stomach or bowels. Constable Angus, not realising how dangerous this man was, tried to take him into custody and in the scuffle, Smith pulled out a sharp shoemaker's knife and stabbed the police officer in the chest and left thigh. Witnesses who had come to assist the police officer grabbed hold of Alexander and took him to the police office. Others took the wounded police officer to the infirmary. The *North British Daily Mail* of Tuesday, 1 June 1858, stated that his wounds were progressing favourably but unfortunately

---

* The newspapers reporting the crime referred to the accused as Alex Tissot. At the trial, Smith was the name used, although the name used in other records is Thomas Smith.

the officer's injuries became infected and he died five days later.

Smith stood in the dock at the High Court in Edinburgh on 19 July 1858. Two doctors, Dr Littlejohn and Dr Simpson (a physician at the jail), stated that they both thought he was insane and not fit to instruct counsel for his defence. Dr Simpson said that the prisoner had violent feelings towards his wife. The prisoner also believed that he was dead and that if he had a knife, he would prove it to the doctor by ripping open his chest and stomach and showing that there was nothing but soot there.

Dr Simpson told the court that Smith explained to him that his wife had confessed to having killed two other men. Smith became convinced that if he did not kill his wife, she would go on to kill others. He told the doctor that if every woman killed two or three men, what would the country do for soldiers, how would it be protected?

The accused also stated that he had been in great pain since his wife had poisoned him and had neither brains nor stomach. Dr Simpson did state, however, that he believed the prisoner did know right from wrong. The accused told him a story that while at sea he had been attacked by a Portuguese sailor. The prisoner said he did not try and retaliate as he knew that when the ship got to port, the Portuguese seafarer would be tried and punished.

Charles Reilly, a prisoner who had shared a jail cell with Alexander Smith, stated that the man in the dock did consider himself dead. Agitated, Smith shouted, 'Not dead but dying'. He also said he did not care what happened to him as he would not be alive to be hanged. Smith also confessed to sometimes being irritable, especially when hungry. He added, 'I am hungry now, I wish I had something to eat. I could eat an old donkey. My blood is all gone and there is nothing but rotten flesh and skin and bone upon me'.

Despite these witness statements, it was not clear as to the prisoner's real state of mind. The next witness, Dr Skae, was the medical superintendent of the Morningside Asylum. Brought forward to give evidence, Dr Skae had his doubts. He stated that for a few days after his arrest the prisoner had been under his charge during which time Smith had tried to persuade the doctor that he was mad, which according to Dr Skae is not what real madmen do. Dr Skae thought Smith was faking his illness.

Another doctor seemed to back this. Dr Renaud practised in the Haydock Lodge Asylum in Lancashire. Dr Renaud stated that Smith was sent to the asylum by the county Poor Law authorities in October 1857 and remained there until 25 January 1858. Dr Renaud stated that he did not consider Smith as insane.

With all this confusion and conflicting opinions as to the accused's state of mind, the court decided to let the Solicitor General determine whether the prisoner was fit to stand trial for murder. To this, Smith stated, *'It is a pity to waste time upon me. Why don't you hang me at once?'*.

The court decided that Smith was not fit to stand trial and recommended that he be locked up in the Morningside Asylum with a clause that if he did ever make a recovery, he would stand trial for the killing of Police Constable Charles Angus.

XI
Police Constable Robert Campbell
City of Glasgow Police

5 November 1863

Just after 9pm on the night of Wednesday, 4 November 1863, two young women, Elizabeth Ferguson and Elizabeth Campbell, locked the door of the fruit shop they worked in at Glassford Street, Glasgow. The women took the key to give to their boss's wife, Mrs Brown, who lived at 39 Stockwell Street, a short walk away, towards the River Clyde.

The two women arrived at the address, walked into the pitch black close and started up the stairs. They got about halfway up the first flight of the spiral staircase when Ferguson's foot hit something soft in the darkness. She let out a scream and her companion behind, thinking it was a joke, pushed her in the back. Ferguson fell over what she took to be a person lying down on the stone steps. She screamed again, hurriedly got to her feet and the two now hysterical women ran down the stairs and out onto the street.

Luckily, Police Constable Robert Campbell happened to be passing along at the other side of Stockwell Street. When he saw the two approaching women, he greeted them with the words, *'Hello, miss, what's ado with you?'*.

STOCKWELL STREET, GLASGOW

Officer Campbell escorted the two women across the road and up the close of 39 Stockwell Street. With the aid of his police lantern, they could see a man sitting on the stairs. The constable said to the stranger, *'Hello, what are you doing there? That's a strange place to be sitting'*.

The officer told the two women that he could deal with the situation and should go. They later related in court that the police officer spoke civilly to the man. One flight up, a Mrs Fullarton was at home helping her grandson who lived with her with his homework. She had heard Ferguson scream and had looked out and down the stairs, but it was too dark to see anything. A short while later, she again heard a noise and this time when she investigated, she saw a police officer holding a lantern speaking to a man sitting on the stairs.

Minutes later, Fullarton heard a lantern falling and something hitting her front door. She opened the door and saw a police officer lying on his back just outside on the landing, his head inches from where her door was. Sitting on top of the officer with his hands around the police officer's neck was a big man; he was strangling Constable Campbell. This brave woman who was described as elderly and was old enough to have a ten-year-old grandson, yelled at the man attacking the constable, 'You villain, are you going to kill the policeman? If you do not let him be, I will get the poker and break your arm'.

Fullarton did not fetch the poker for she wisely realised that if the attacker got hold of it, he could use it as a weapon against the constable, herself and her grandson. Instead, she tried to grapple with the man and pull him from the police officer. She received blows to the legs and chest. Somehow, she still managed to distract the man, allowing the police officer to crawl into her house. As the pair struggled, he said to her, 'It's not you I would hurt, but it's him I want to be at'. She joined the police officer and they shut the man out. They waited a couple of minutes at which time they heard the man head down the stairs.

The householder gave the shaken and bruised Campbell a drink of water. As he was sure the man had left the building, the police officer walked down the stairs. Fullarton heard a further struggle and someone shout, 'Murder!'.

Fullarton ran up the stairs, desperately banging on all the doors, trying to get someone to assist the police officer again under attack. No one opened their door to her cries for help. Running back down the staircase, she saw a couple of men at the foot of the steps. She called to them, 'Will you stand there and see a policeman killed?'.

With no one willing to get involved, Campbell shouted to Fullarton to go to the spirit shop next door and get the owner, a Mr Gallacher. As the police officer fought for his life, he managed to give his whistle to a man watching. This man went into the street and blew for assistance. Two police officers on patrol answered this call for help. The officers grabbed the man attacking Campbell and marched him off to the police station.

Campbell was shaken and complaining of having a sore leg which he thought may be broken and he had a nasty lump on his forehead. The officer wearily went up the stairs looking for his lost lantern. A brief time later, some colleagues found Campbell, slumped semi-conscious on the stairwell. Dr McGill, who checked over the officer, thought the wounds were not severe and ordered someone to take the police officer home.

Robert Campbell, who had been in the force since 1850 and described as a quiet and well-behaved officer, died at 7am the following morning. He was forty-six years of age and left a wife and six children to mourn his loss.

The police identified the man responsible for Officer Campbell's death as Alexander Graham. He lived in Soho Street, which ran between the Gallowgate and Crownpoint Road (the western building of St Mungo's Academy now stands on what was once Soho Street). While locked up following his arrest, Graham had been aggressive and excited, showing signs of being drunk.

Graham told the officers investigating the attack that he had been a soldier in the 78th Highland Regiment but had been pensioned out and was now a weaver. He stated that on the day of his attack he had gone to the bank and withdrawn £1/12/–. He spent the rest of the time drinking in taverns in Stockwell Street, the High Street and in the Bridgegate area. The prisoner admitted being drunk and admitted to having no recollection of attacking the police officer. While in custody he seemed remorseful about his part in the police officer's death.

Graham was tried for murder at the High Court in Glasgow on 23 December 1863. After the witnesses for the prosecution had given an account of the events leading to Campbell's death, witnesses gave an insight as to the character of the accused man.

Robert McFarlane stated that he had served with the prisoner in the army in India for seventeen years. McFarlane vouched that the accused was a steady, good soldier. He also stated that he had not heard of his being quarrelsome in drink. McFarlane also told the court the man on trial had received two good conduct badges while in the military. Another ex-soldier, James Ormiston, described Graham as a quiet, inoffensive man.

There seems to have been a dispute as to the exact cause of Constable Campbell's death. Doctors Stewart and Macleod conducted the post-mortem; they agreed that the officer's death was blood on the brain and the violent attack was the most probable cause. Dr Guthrie, however, thought that his death might have been due to excitement. It is worth quoting directly from Dr James Morton, a member for the Faculty of Physicians and Surgeons in Glasgow as it gives an idea of the conflicting medical opinions. Dr Morton said at the trial:

I have heard the evidence in this case, and have heard the medical report. I find nothing in the internal appearance there described inconsistent with death from natural apoplexy. From that medical report I would not be inclined to say that there is any necessary connection between the marks on the head and the effusion on the brain. The place where the blood was found in the tissues of the brain would favour the idea that death resulted from natural causes. Excitement in a person predisposed to apoplexy is one of the immediate causes of it. The state of Campbell's heart and lungs renders it probable that he would have died from great excitement, irrespective of violence.

With the confusion as to the cause of death, the Advocate-Deputy withdrew the charge of murder. The Crown now sought the lesser charge of manslaughter. The jury retired and after a brief absence of around fifteen minutes returned to give a guilty verdict with a recommendation of mercy. Alexander Graham was sentenced to ten-years' penal service.

XII
Police Constable Thomas Mutch
Edinburgh City Police

1 December 1868

A loud disturbance in the Grassmarket attracted Kenneth McRae of the Edinburgh City Police in the early hours of 17 November 1868. Four men were fooling around, play-fighting and making a noise. McRae would later state he ordered them to quieten down and go home to bed. One of the men turned and started walking up the stairs of a close on the south side of the market. Two of the men quietened down and stood aside, but the fourth man continued to shout and swear, threatening to report the police officer to the Superintendent. McRae, who had only been in the force for six months must have felt relieved when another police officer, Thomas Mutch, appeared on the scene.

The two police constables grabbed hold of this man and dragged him across the pavement; the officers told the protesting man they were arresting him for breach of the peace. The man started to struggle with the officers. A woman came down the stairs and explained that she was the struggling man's wife and pleaded for his release saying that she would take him home. The officers asked the man if he would go home should they let him go? He replied, 'No'. The situation escalated when his friends tried to help the man under arrest. One of them pushed Constable McRae down. The man who had started to go up the stairs turned around and rushed into the street. Carrying a poker, he struck McRae, who was getting to his feet, over the head. He turned and hit Mutch on the face or head. Then three of the men ran away in the direction of the Cowgate.

Dazed, McRae walked over to see to Mutch. He saw that the injured officer was on his hands and knees with blood pouring from his nose and eyes. He complained of being blind and he could hardly walk. Mutch was taken to Edinburgh Royal Infirmary where he died in the days after the attack. McRae was off work for a week with his injuries.

POLICE BOX, COWGATE, EDINBURGH

The police arrested the four men involved. They were John McCabe, Francis Ward, Michael Ward and David Hume. Three of these men appeared in Edinburgh High Court on 1 February 1868. The Lord Advocate decided not to charge McCabe, but to charge both Wards for assault and murder. Francis Ward pled not guilty, stating that he was not there at the time of the police officer's death. Michael Ward said that it was David Hume who had dealt the fatal blow that night.

Officer McRae verified that the men on trial were those involved in the attack. He stated that it was Michael Ward who resisted arrest but named McCabe as being the man who struck him and Constable Mutch with a poker. This statement was the start of conflicting and confusing reports.

Hume was brought forward as a witness for the prosecution. Hume appears to have turned Queen's evidence. As he stood in the witness stand to give his account of the police officer's death, Lord Ardmillan said to Hume, *'I have to tell you that you are now safe from prosecution on the ground of this offence. You cannot be punished for any share you may have had in it yourself, but it is your duty to speak the whole truth'.* Hume told the court that he and McCabe were standing at the foot of their stairs and that Michael Ward was standing at the bottom of his stairs. The distance between the stairs was about fifteen or twenty yards. Hume stated that the three of them were having a laugh when Officer McRae walked up to them and told them to get off to bed. The witness also claimed that McCabe answered the officer by saying he was going to bed and turned to set off up the steps. Then the police officer stepped up the stairs and grabbed McCabe, calling him a scoundrel. The two men struggled and fell down the steps onto the street, both landing on their backs. Hume stated that Michael Ward's sister, Bridget Ward was there and witnessed this. Hume also said that he knew Francis Ward but denied he was there at the time. Hume went on to say that McCabe demanded to understand why the police officer attacked him and threatened to report Constable McRae. He noted that Mutch joined the other constable and both officers dragged McCabe across the pavement towards the street. Hume then testified that Michael Ward struck the police officer with the poker, claiming, Michael struck McRae over the head, turned around and threw the poker at Mutch. Hume said the sharp end of the poker hit the officer in the eye.

The court now had to deal with the fact that the police officer's evidence was entirely at odds with that of Hume, who now had protection from prosecution. McRae stated that it was Michael Ward who was placed under arrest for breach of the peace, and McCabe who had attacked the officers with a poker. Hume stated that it was McCabe who was being arrested. Michael Ward struck the police officers. To add to the confusion Michael Ward's defence argued that it was not him who attacked the constables, but Hume, who had immunity and could not be brought to charge.

Another witness, a lodging housekeeper in the Grassmarket,

Alex Campbell, told the court that he looked out of his window and saw McCabe and McRae struggling on the ground. Campbell stated that he did not see anyone strike the police officer. He did say that he saw both McCabe and Michael Ward but did not see Francis Ward at the scene.

The next witness did little to clear up the confusion as to who hit the constables. Mr Wallace was a clerk in the office of the Procurator Fiscal's; he had gone to the infirmary to get a statement from Constable Mutch, the officer who was lying injured and would soon die from his injuries. Wallace stated that the stricken police officer had told him it was Francis Ward who struck the officers with the poker.

The next witness was Bridget Ward, the sister of Francis and Michael. She stated that on the night in question a cry of '*Oh John, go quietly with the police*' awoke her. Bridget got dressed and went out into the Grassmarket. She saw Mrs McCabe running towards her with a poker in her hand and she also noticed a police officer lying on the ground. Mrs McCabe handed her the poker and said, '*Bridget, hide that*'. She gave it to a Mary McLevy who she said slept with her. Mary threw the poker away. Bridget also told the court that she did not see Francis Ward that night.

John Robb who was a lodging housekeeper in the Grassmarket, stated that Francis Ward and his wife stayed in his lodging house. The Wards shared a room with another two couples, the Hills and Smiths. Robb said he saw Francis Ward that night between 8pm and 9pm but admitted the door was unlocked. When the attack on the officers took place, both William Smith (a blacksmith) and John Hill (a chair mender), testified that Francis Ward was in the room lying in bed.

Lord Ardmillan summed up and told the jury that all the evidence pointed to the fact that during the attack on the officers, Francis Ward was not at the scene. He pointed out that both policemen's statements had offered different names as to who the attacker was. Ardmillan also stated that Michael Ward had indicated that it was not he but David Hume who struck the officers, but no witness had backed this up. The judge advised that if anything this was a case of culpable homicide.

The jury retired and after twenty minutes returned with a verdict of not proven against Michael Ward; Francis Ward was found not guilty. The court dropped the charges against John McCabe, freeing all three prisoners. No one was ever convicted for killing Police Constable Thomas Mutch.

XIII
Inspector Lachlan McKinnon
Greenock Burgh Police

1 January 1869

Robert Simpson was working in his confectionary shop at 33 Hamilton Street, Greenock, on 1 January 1869 when a drunk entered the premises. Simpson was to remember him being medium height with sharp features and clean-shaven except under the chin. The man asked Simpson if he would sell him beer. Simpson stated that he did not sell beer. The man opened a door and walked into Simpson's private living quarters. The shopkeeper came from behind the counter and went after the man. Once again, he was asked for and refused to sell beer and at that the man suddenly struck the shopkeeper, hitting him full in the face and knocking out two of Simpson's front teeth, saying as he lashed out, '*Take that!*'.

The shopkeeper reeled backwards, clutching his injured mouth. A young man, John Thomson, was in the shop and upon seeing the assault said to the man, '*You should not abuse the man that way*'. Thomson also told Simpson that he should call for the police. The man went to strike the shopkeeper again and Thomson received a blow to his right arm when he stepped in front of Simpson. Thomson grabbed the man's arm and the two men struggled before the intruder broke free and fled eastwards along the street with Thomson in hot pursuit. While this was happening, Simpson ran into the road and got hold of two police officers.

The shopkeeper and the police officers caught up with Thomson and the man as they were grappling in the street. As the police officers approached, a spectator yelled at them, *'Take care, that man has a knife'*. Inspector Lachlan McKinnon grabbed the man on the shoulder. The man turned around and plunged a knife into the inspector's neck. As he ran away, McKinnon cried, *'Catch that man, I am done for!'*.

Thomson again gave chase and managed to trip the fleeing man, holding him until the police turned up and took him into custody. A large crowd had assembled outside the confectionery shop and some of them carried the stricken officer into a nearby drug shop and laid him on the counter where he died a few minutes later. Inspector McKinnon was thirty-seven and left a wife and young family. He was described as a most intelligent officer, and remarkable for his quiet disposition. It was also said of him that he was well known and much esteemed not only by his fellow officers but by all who knew him.

When Thomson got up, he noticed blood pouring down his arm and when he got home, he realised he had been stabbed in the arm and twice in the leg. Later that evening, the police found a knife with a black handle at the scene of the crime. The man responsible was twenty-four-year-old James Gallin an 'iron' shipbuilder – a plater for Messrs Caird & Co, where he worked alongside a married brother*. Gallin was from County Donegal (newspapers reported that he was born in America to Irish parents). On 4 January 1869, *The Dundee Courier* called him an *'Irish Yankee'* and claimed that Gallin had been a sailor. He was alleged to have survived the wrecking of the steamship *Hibernia*, although the *Courier* pointed out that his name was not on the list of the ship's crew. Gallin had been working in Greenock for three years until his arrest, staying in a lodging house in Tobago Street. He was engaged to a young woman who lived in Clark's Land which stood at the head of Anne Street.

Gallin was tried at the High Court in Glasgow on 21 April 1869.

---

* James Gallin is also referred to as James Gillan in reports.

John Thomson was called to give evidence and stated what he had witnessed in the shop. He also told of chasing Gallin and struggling with him. Thomson talked of seeing the prisoner strike Inspector McKinnon in the neck. Thomson explained to the court that he did not feel the stab wounds at the time. It was only after the excitement had died down that he noticed that he was himself injured. Thomson thought it was during the first altercation in the shop that his injuries occurred.

Eyewitnesses to the assault gave evidence to the court. Alexander Allan, a sawyer, was going to the theatre on the evening of the attack. He stated that at about 6.30pm on 1 January 1869 he witnessed a 'row' in Simpson's shop. Allan saw Gallin struggle with Thomson and the inspector receive a blow to the left ear which caused the blood to flow. Allan then told of hearing McKinnon call, '*Some of ye catch him now, I am done for!*'.

John Mitchell Beren, a clothier and outfitter, gave a statement in which he said he remembered seeing two men wrestling beside Simpson's shop. Inspector McKinnon then came along. Gallin gave a sweeping blow behind McKinnon's left ear, and blood spurted out from the wound. The prisoner hesitated for a minute, looked at him in a confused manner before turning and rapidly running up the street. Beren alleged that as the police officer collapsed, he tried to catch him but as he fell the officer turned and someone else grabbed the wounded man.

Next to be called to give evidence were Doctors Auld and Shortridge. Both doctors had conducted the post-mortem and told of a wound in the victim's neck, below the left ear. This puncture was about three inches deep and had severed an artery. The injury was caused by a sharp-pointed instrument, driven with considerable force. The doctors agreed that due to severe loss of blood, death must have come quickly to the unfortunate police officer.

In a statement read to the court, Gallin admitted to being drunk on the afternoon on 1 January. He did not remember using a knife on anyone that night. He admitted owning a knife for cutting tobacco but stated his knife had a white handle and not a black one like that produced as evidence.

Margaret Gillespie who owned the lodging house in Tobago Street where Gallin lived, stated that she had given him a knife which, to the best of her knowledge, had a black handle. However, Gillespie could not identify the knife in court as the one she had given the accused.

Witnesses were brought forward by the defence to testify as to the excellent character of the man in the dock. After the judge summed up, the jury retired to consider all the evidence. Twenty minutes later, the jury returned with a statement of guilty of culpable homicide, and James Gallin was sentenced to twenty years of penal servitude.

XIV
Police Constable James Fraser
Elginshire Constabulary

19 July 1878

On 17 July 1878, Alexander Fraser stood on the platform of Grantown-on-Spey railway station waiting for the southbound train to arrive from Inverness. At noon, as Fraser watched the train approach, something unusual caught his attention. Around three people were on the top of the coal bunker on the tender of the train. They seemed to be holding another man down. Fraser was surprised to see that the restrained man was well-known local farmer Andrew Granger.

Granger was taken from the train and spoke to Fraser. The farmer acted strangely; he said to Fraser that he thought there were people out to hurt him and seemed to believe he was in danger. Granger also complained of having the feeling that his tongue was burning. Fraser, who was employed by the Grant Arms Hotel to drive a carriage from the station to the hotel, left to go to the hotel and Granger remained at the station.

Granger was then himself taken to the Grant Arms and again he met Alexander Fraser in the hotel bar. He was still acting oddly, convinced he was in danger and saying to Fraser, '*I have known you for a long time, and I hope you will not allow anyone to do me any harm*'. When asked if Granger was going to continue his journey south, the anxious and confused man said, '*No*'. He asked if he could have the quietest room in the hotel so he could rest. Fraser took Granger up to Room 18. Granger wanted the door locked and asked Fraser to look under the bed to make sure no one was hiding there. Once the farmer was satisfied that he was alone, Fraser left the room. As he walked out the door, Fraser heard the door lock behind him.

Sometime later, a maid came running up to Fraser. She told him of a commotion coming from Number 18. Fraser ran up the stairs and heard a great noise from the room. Knocking on the door, Fraser asked Granger what was happening in the bedroom. The farmer replied that '*He was making gallows to hang them all*'. When asked to open the door, Granger refused. A maid told him that the deranged man had knocked out a window and she feared that he was planning to jump. To break the man's fall should he jump, the hotel staff placed mattresses on the ground. Fraser rushed off to find a police officer.

James Fraser who was one of the local constables, made his way up the stairs to Room 18. He knocked on the door and asked to be let in, saying, '*Will you not open the door, Mr Granger? I know you and your brother quite well*'. Granger refused this request. Opening the door with a spare key, the police officer and the hotel employee, Alexander Fraser, rushed in. Granger was behind the door and in the confusion, Fraser heard the police officer cry out in pain and fall back. Realising that the constable was injured, Alexander Fraser dragged the police officer out of the room. When asked as to the extent of his injuries, Constable Fraser said, '*I am stabbed, and I fear I am done for*'. The stricken police officer removed his hand covering the wound. It was clear the injury was severe as foodstuff wept out of the wound. The police officer was helped down the stairs by Alexander Fraser and a maid.

THE GRANT ARMS HOTEL, GRANTOWN ON SPEY

The police officer was laid out on a couch downstairs and then taken home. Meanwhile, Alexander Fraser and a small crowd of people including the stationmaster, Mr Forbes, went back to Granger's room. They tried to push open the door, but Granger was putting his weight to the other side. Knowing him to be armed and dangerous, the men used a long pole to push open the door. Granger was overpowered and taken out of the room. The authorities did not find a knife. A passing boy discovered one lying outside, tossed from the window. Granger was taken to the police office shouting, '*Murder!*'. Fraser was to die from his wounds at home on 19 July, two days after the stabbing.

Granger was tried for murder at the Inverness Circuit Court on Friday, 13 September 1878. The night before the trial, Judge Lord Deas arrived by train from Aberdeen. He was met on the platform by the Provost and magistrates of Inverness. The Inverness Militia formed a guard of honour.

Granger pled not guilty to murder, arguing that at the time of the Fraser's killing he was insane. It became clear that Granger was acting strangely on the day of the stabbing. Forbes, the stationmaster, said that when Granger left the train, he asked to see a doctor. At the hotel, a doctor examined him. The confused man believed the doctor might try to poison him. The court heard that while in custody, Granger had had a loud discussion with his wife, but she was not there. The prisoner's thirteen-year-old daughter told the court that the day before the killing, Granger had attended the Wool Fair at Inverness. He had been drinking heavily at the fair and that night while at home Granger was acting strangely. She said that her father was afraid that there was someone else in the house. He had her fetch a sword that hung in the hall and Granger slept that night with the sword by his side. She told the court that days before the killing of the police officer, her father had been ill in bed and unable to eat. A distiller, John McGregor, told of talking to Granger at Grantown station. He said that Granger spoke of receiving a fright on the train; the farmer pointing to his heart stated that this fright was one that he should never forget. The witness said that Granger's chest was heaving, and he was extremely excited but did not appear to be drunk.

While held in Elgin Prison, Granger was still showing signs of mental illness, telling Governor George Donaldson that he could see horses, sheep and cattle coming out of the ventilators. Donaldson recounted to the court that Granger was trying to catch them. Granger told Donaldson that he knew nothing about the events surrounding the stabbing of the officer. John Chapman, a police officer at Elgin, stated that Granger seemed bemused as to why he should be locked up and did not appreciate the seriousness of the crime he had committed.

The main issue was to establish whether Granger was insane at the time of the killing or suffering the effects of alcohol. He admitted excessive drinking at the Wool Fair the day before the murder and on the morning of the police officer's death. The doctors and witnesses who testified as to the prisoner's state of mind convinced the Crown that Granger should face the lesser charge of culpable homicide.

The jury found Granger guilty. The prisoner received a sentence of five-years' penal servitude. The judge told the prisoner that if he were only suffering from the effects of alcohol, he would be guilty of murder. After reading out the sentence, Lord Deans said to Granger that if in the future the prisoner would totally abstain from drink, he might yet be a prosperous man. It is a shame that Constable James Fraser did not have a chance to prosper himself.

XV
Police Constable George Low
Edinburgh City Police

14 March 1881

Alexander Rintoul, a house painter, was working in his workshop at 10pm on the night of 14 March 1881. Suddenly his wife appeared in a state of distress and bid Alexander to come with her to their house in Union Place, Edinburgh. When the couple got home, Alexander saw his son David Rintoul standing with his hand in a basin of red water. The young man's hand was bleeding heavily. Alexander understandably asked his son as to how he had injured himself. David nodded towards another young man in the house, John Henry Shewan, and told his father that Shewan had accidentally stabbed him injuring his hand. The older man inspected the wound and saw a deep cut between the thumb and forefinger. After treating his son's hand, Alexander asked the men to explain what had happened.

David told his parents that he and John had decided to see someone who lived in 1 Elm Row. The two young men were both sailors on leave, serving aboard the Royal Navy gunboat HMS *Vigilant*, which was docked in Granton Harbour. After visiting their friend, they were making their way down the staircase and David decided to find the water closet (communal toilet). To get there, David had to go down to the bottom of the stairs, out into the back of the tenement building and through a gate. This gate led into an enclosed area behind the shops facing the street. While David was searching for someplace to relieve himself, Shewan waited in the dark stairway.

Shewan suddenly heard two men struggling down the stairs. He ran down into the basement and saw a police officer had grabbed his friend and the two men were grappling. Shewan took out a dagger and plunged it into the police officer's back repeatedly, a blow of which injured David's hand. As the officer staggered back and released his grip, David ripped a loose iron railing from a fence and struck the officer with it. The two men fled the scene and made their way to Union Place. The older man was horrified by what he had just heard. Shewan said that he had not meant to hurt 'Davie' and seemed extremely concerned about what his grandmother would think of him when told what he had done. Shewan said he planned to flee the city, but Alexander persuaded him to stay and face the music. Alexander left his son and his friend in the house with his wife, while with what must have been a heavy heart, he walked to the police station at St James Street and reported the incident.

ROYAL NAVY GUNBOAT HMS *VIGILANT*

Dispatched to investigate, Sergeant William Andrew realised that Elm Row was on Constable George Low's beat, as a bakery had been broken into the previous September. Low's duties required him to regularly check the back of those premises. When Andrew arrived at the scene of the crime, he found Low lying face down on the stairs. Low was still clutching his baton; his smashed lamp and an iron bar were lying close to his dead body. During a search of the area, the police found a chisel stuffed behind a barrel. Andrew left a couple of constables at the scene and went with a Sergeant Mackay to Union Place to speak to the two young men involved. When the police officers turned up, Shewan asked if the police officer was much hurt. When told that the officer was dead, he cried out, 'My God, what is to be done?'.

David said to his friend, 'You know Henry, I didn't stab him – I struck him with the iron railing on the breast'. After Shewan admitted stabbing the officer five times, he was arrested. The police decided to leave David as a doctor who assessed the injured hand thought him to be in a weak state due to loss of blood.

Dr Littlejohn inspected the body of the dead police officer. The deceased was twenty-two, a native of Tillyfourie, near Alford in Aberdeenshire, and had only been in the force between two and three years when killed. Officer Low had eleven stab wounds, mostly to his back, but two were in his chest near the heart. Low also had an injury to the head, caused by being hit by the iron railing. A dagger was found which had a brass handle and a seven-inch blade. David denied knowing that Shewan was carrying a knife. He stated that he initially thought a bite by the police officer during the struggle had caused the wound to his hand. Shewan readily admitted to stabbing the officer.

As the police investigated the crime, the story the two sailors gave did not ring true: there was no one living in Elm Row who knew or had received a visit from the accused on the night of 14 March. The Edinburgh Evening News, dated the day after the killing of the officer on 15 March, stated the chisel found was like a jemmy used by burglars. David Rintoul also had form, having been convicted in 1877 for housebreaking.

Charged with killing officer Low, David Rintoul and John Henry Shewan pled not guilty in front of a packed courtroom at the High Court in Edinburgh on 13 June 1881.

ELM ROW AND HADDINGTON PLACE, EDINBURGH

The state of the gate leading to the cellar, whether it had been secure or left unlocked, confused the court with different accounts given. John MacIntosh, a porter who worked in a grocer's shop in Elm Row, stated that at 10am on the day of the killing he was down in the basement and he thought the gate was closed but not locked. Lauchlan Sinclair, a pastrycook who worked in a bakers and confectioners at 2 Elm Row, said that when he went down at 6am on 14 March the door was locked, and he had to use a key to open it. Elizabeth Dickson, a housekeeper to a tenant at 2 Elm Row, also stated that the door leading into the basement area was locked. The state of the gate was an essential matter because if the door was unlocked, David may have gained access while engaged in looking for a toilet, a harmless and legitimate act. If the gate was locked, however, David would have had to force his way past the door. The prosecution produced evidence that the chisel was used to force a way into the basement. Inspector James Christie told the court that he had inspected the door. Marks he found on the post opposite the lock did precisely fit the chisel. Christie said that the marks were fresh, especially where a bit of wood had been wrenched away from the post. The inspector thought that it was quite evident that the marks had been made to force open the door.

Andrew Lawrensen, an apprentice joiner, told the court that Shewan had asked for a loan of a chisel. Shewan made model ships and Lawrensen thought this tool was for that purpose. Lawrensen's sister, Cecilia, backed her brother's statement as she saw her brother hand the chisel over to the accused and Cecilia said Shewan passed it to David as he had bigger pockets. Cecilia also understood that Shewan needed the tool for model-making. Mr Lawrensen Snr verified this, for he also saw his son hand over the chisel to Shewan. When asked about blood found on the handle of the chisel, Andrew Lawrensen stated that the blood was there when he gave Shewan the woodworking tool.

The case rested on whether the two accused had gone to Elm Row intending to commit a robbery or gone to pay a visit to a friend. The men in the dock stated that they were in the vicinity visiting an acquaintance. Shewan said that he had a dagger made for him by this friend in Elm Row and wanted him to make the blade thinner. James Aird, an apprentice plummer (lead worker), stated that he had lived at Elm Row up until the previous March and he confirmed that he had been asked by Shewan to make him a dagger. However, Aird confessed that he saw Shewan the day before Low's death and the accused had never mentioned getting his dagger blade adjusted.

Was this a tragic accident, a case of Shewan seeing a man attack his friend in the dark while the two of them were going about their lawful business? Certainly, Shewan seemed to have used excessive force in freeing his pal from the clutches of Constable Low. The officer was wearing his uniform greatcoat and underneath that he had on another coat and a soldier's jacket beneath that, then two thick flannel shirts and a vest. The knife inflicted the wounds with such force as to penetrate all the clothing. The officer had sixteen wounds on his body when found. The prosecution argued that these two young men, Shewan (who was only seventeen at the time of his trial) and Rintoul (who was eighteen), had intended to commit a crime. If discovered, they had taken a dagger along with them to fend off arrest. If this was the case, both must be found guilty of murder, no matter who had wielded the killer blows.

The defence argued that the two men were caught up in a tragic circumstance and both had acted out of character. While David was struggling with the police officer, Shewan had a rush of blood to the head and was only guilty of culpable homicide, with David being guilty of assault. The jury retired to consider the case but returned after only 15 minutes with a verdict of culpable homicide against Shewan and a charge of assault against David Rintoul. Four days later, John Henry Shewan received fifteen-years' penal servitude and David Rintoul received an eighteen-month prison sentence.

XVI
Police Constable David McDonald
Leith Burgh Police

20 June 1882

As Police Constable David McDonald of the Leith Burgh Police was walking on his beat on Leith Shore on the night of 24 May 1882, he came upon Patrick Smith, a labourer. Smith was drunk, noisy and causing a disturbance. McDonald grabbed Smith and whilst he was holding the struggling Smith, he blew his whistle and waited for assistance to arrive. The man resisting arrest took out a small knife and stabbed the constable in the left leg. Struggling and in pain, McDonald hit Smith over the head with his baton.

When the knife was later found its tip was missing. Smith admitted owning the weapon, stating he used it for cutting tobacco. As the wound was not considered severe, the court charged Smith with breach of the peace. Smith claimed to have stabbed the police officer while defending himself after being struck with the baton; his bandaged head wound was offered as evidence of Smith's claim. Nonetheless, Smith was found guilty and fined five shillings or three days of imprisonment at the Sheriff Court. The judge criticised Officer McDonald for the overzealous use of his baton.

A doctor had attended both men after the assault. The doctor, aware the tip of the knife was missing, looked inside the wound, and not finding any trace of the knifepoint, he assumed it had broken off and was lying in the street at the Shore. McDonald had his injury treated in hospital and was then sent home. Just two weeks later McDonald's leg was showing signs of infection. The police officer went to the infirmary where a surgeon found the tip of the knife embedded in the bone below the officer's knee. McDonald returned home. Six days later, he was back in the hospital with blood poisoning. Constable David McDonald was described as a highly intelligent constable and of trustworthy and discreet disposition and much liked by his brother officers. He died on 20 June 1882.

PERTH SHERIFF COURT

The police rearrested Smith and held him on a charge of murder. But there were questions: could they charge Smith? At that time, a person could not be charged twice for the same crime. The *Leith Burghs Pilot* of 24 June 1882 reported that as he had pled guilty to a charge of breach of the peace, Smith could not be charged with murder:

I have not been able to find any record of a murder trial in connection to Patrick Smith. Perhaps it was decided that he could not face a new charge under the double jeopardy law. The authorities might have feared that as Smith was severely injured and stated that the policeman had hit him first, it might be tough to get a conviction. Whatever the reason, it seems Smith was not tried for murder.

David McDonald was originally from Caithness and at a council meeting it was decided that the Burghs of Leith should pay to return the body to the officer's family. McDonald's remains were taken under an escort of fifty police officers to the Albert Dock and put on the steamer *St Magnus*, which took McDonald home for burial amongst his own kin.

Just six days after the death of Police Constable David McDonald, another police officer received a stab wound in Glasgow. A young lad, Patrick McDermid, stabbed the officer in the neck while the police officer dispersed a noisy crowd in the city's King Street.

XVII
Police Constable Alexander Lamond
Kirkcaldy Burgh Police

26 May 1883

Police Constables Alexander Lamond and Robert Mays were on patrol walking their beat in the Fife town of Kirkcaldy on the night of 25 May 1883. It was a Friday and as is still often the case for the Scottish police force, one of the busiest nights of the week. The police heard of a noisy disturbance taking place in a house in the Harbour Head area. A young millworker, Jane Murdoch, occupied the house.

As they approached the house at 11pm, the officers could hear a great deal of noise emerging from the building. This complaint had been one of a number in the last few weeks regarding noise coming from this house which stood between a cluster of bonded warehouses and the Harbour Head Hotel. It was clear that there were people in the building and, by the sound of it, were drinking and had, as is said in Scotland, a skin fu (full of drink or drunk). When the officers entered the house, they found a group shouting and arguing noisily amongst themselves. The two police officers spent a full ten minutes trying to get the occupants to quieten and calm down. The drunks turned their anger on the two officers. It became clear that things were now getting out of hand and the drinkers were becoming increasingly aggressive towards the police officers. Constable Lamond instructed his colleague to fetch reinforcements. When Officer Mays left, Lamond who was only twenty-seven, bravely stood in front of the door with his truncheon in hand, barring any escape.

Lamond was attacked as he stood in front of the door. The attackers ripped the officer's baton from his hand and used it against him. They also hit him with a fire fender and a crossbar taken from a chair. The drunks struck Lamond repeatedly until he fell to the ground. Then the mob kicked and stamped the police officer lying on the floor. When the assault was over, Lamond managed to get up and stumble from the house into the street. There he collapsed into the arms of a bystander. The injured officer was taken to the nearby Harbour Head Hotel and it was there that the young police officer from Deeside died from his injuries.

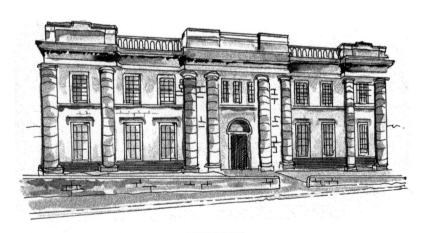

CUPAR JAIL

72

In the subsequent search for those involved, the police arrested four men in a house in Hill Place, Kirkcaldy. Taken and locked up in Cupar Jail were brothers James and Alexander Young (aged thirty and twenty-seven respectively), Charles McGuinness (aged thirty-three) and John Doig. They were all hawkers (travelling salespeople) from the Aberdeen area. Also incarcerated was Jane Murdoch, along with another two women who had been in her house when the officer died.

Doig was quickly released when it became apparent that he had tried to stop the assault, as were the women who did not take part in the attack on Lamond. The remaining three men, James and Alexander Young and Charles McGuinness, stood in the dock at the Perth Circuit Court on 6 July 1883, charged with murder.

The *Fife Free Press, & Kirkcaldy Guardian* wrote for the following day's issue that, '*Charles McGuinness dressed in a light brown suit, his face an expression of indifference, when asked to plea, spoke in a loud firm voice*'. The same reporter, when speaking about the Young brothers stated, '*James Young was dressed in a suit of light grey tweeds. He wore a look of ill-concealed anxiety, spoke in an undertone, and seemed much relieved when asked to sit down*'; and that his brother Alexander seemed, '*the most anxious of the three*'.

The newspaper also stated that the Crown had twenty-eight witnesses and interestingly reported, '*But the evidence of more than one-half of those would have been of little consequence*'. This statement indicates the questionable quality of the witnesses. A report by the two doctors who conducted the post-mortem stated that Lamond had died from a brain haemorrhage due to being beaten about the head by one or more blunt instruments, resulting in a fracturing of the skull.

Instructed to plead to the charge of murder, the three defendants all stood and one by one stated that they would admit guilt to the lesser charge of culpable homicide. The Advocate Depute accepted this lesser charge, the reason being that the three men in the dock had not set out to murder Lamond that night. When the police officer entered the house in the harbour area of Kirkcaldy, he did not arrest anyone but despite this, he would not let them leave the house. It was argued by the defence counsel that all three of the accused were married family men and their sole motive was not to take the life of the police officer, but to get away from the suspicious locality where they were found. The defence appealed for mercy.

The judge stated that the three men had set about the police officer, attacking him with weapons and using extreme violence, but added:

> *Fortunately for you, there was no previous intent; there was no malice, but just that recklessness from an over-indulgence in the gratification of your passions that led you to inflict such violence that ended in death.*

James and Alexander Young and Charles McGuinness each received a sentence of ten-years' penal servitude. The relieved men who, if found guilty of murder, would certainly have been facing a sentence of death shook hands with each other. When taken down to the cells, a shout from the public gallery of *'Cheer up; keep up your hearts; it will soon wear awa'* could be heard from among those who had turned up to support the prisoners. As the men disappeared down the stairs to the cells, several women rushed forward screaming hysterically and one woman fainted in her seat.

XVIII
Inspector David McBay
Dundee City Police

19 August 1893

At 3.20pm on 15 August 1893, an injured woman ran out into a Dundee street, screaming and shouting that she had been shot by Jack the Ripper. A few moments earlier, the woman, Isabella Norrie, and her daughter Catherine Millar, who lived across the road but had been having tea with her mother, were standing on the third-floor landing talking to their neighbour, Mrs Leckie. They were chatting in a large tenement building in John Street, Dundee. (John Street is now under the Dudhope Roundabout joining the A923 Lochee Road to the A991.) John Fairley, known locally as 'Jack the Ripper' was coming down the stairs; he was going for a walk with his four-year-old son. When the powerfully built former stoker, Fairley, saw the group of women, he accused them of destroying the plaster on the wall. When Isabella stated that the proprietor had told her to pull down the loose plaster, Fairley swore and threatened them before continuing down the stairs. Fairley never made it out onto the street as, his mind racing with injustice and anger, he turned around walked up the stair to the top of the building where he had his room. He fetched a large box out from under his bed, armed himself with a six-chambered revolver, and went back down the stairs to confront the women. As Isabella Norrie stood talking to Mrs Leckie (Catherine had gone back into the house), Fairley drew out the revolver without warning and shot the stunned woman twice, hitting her in the abdomen.

As Isabella ran shouting for help into the street, Catherine came out into the stairwell carrying her week-old infant to see what the noise was. When John saw her, he levelled his pistol shouting, *'Now it's your turn next!'*. He shot her in the abdomen and the right thigh. Mrs Leckie managed to flee indoors. Fairley hurried upstairs to his attic room and locked himself in his top-floor dwelling.

Out in the streets, news of the shootings spread through the town and wide-eyed, excitable people were stopping and exaggerating the events that had taken place in John Street. Tales that Fairley, a pistol in each hand, was shooting anyone he saw, spread through the city. Large crowds, all keen to know just what was happening, descended on the area.

When a crowd of excited boys ran into Central Police Station in West Bell Street and told the officers what had happened, the police must have thought this account exaggerated. Even after a man walked into the office and gave his version of events, the real significance and danger of the situation did not sink in. The police not realising the threat, sent only three police officers to investigate. When they reached John Street, a fourth constable joined them. The four police officers entered the tenement building and ascended the stairs. John Wishart, a civilian, also walked into the building with the officers – he may have known Fairley and believed he could talk him into surrendering.

The crowd out in the street had watched the police enter the building and moments later shots rang out. Wishart stumbled from the building, blood streaming down his right arm and his head bleeding. He walked unaided down the street without uttering a word. Next, Constable John Anderson emerged holding his jaw, shot in the face and arm. Two men escorted Anderson to the nearby infirmary. Another police officer staggered from the building. He was Constable William Dickson and had been shot in the chest, under the right shoulder. Members of the crowd helped Dickson to the police station where a doctor tended to his wounds.

The remaining two police officers now emerged unscathed. They were to tell later that on reaching the top of the stairs they saw Fairley's door was ajar, the point of a gun sticking out. Suddenly and without any warning, Fairley pulled the trigger and fired at the police officers at the top of the stairs. The first shot hit Constable Anderson who fell back into the arms of Constable Clark. Another shot hit Dickson and a bullet flew past Clark's head. Fairley slammed the door shut and drew the bolt, locking it. A force of police officers soon surrounded the building and tried to keep the now vast crowds back out of harm's way.

Things had now settled into a siege as the police encircled the building. The authorities knew that to force an entry might result in further bloodshed. Fairley's young son was also locked in the building. The police feared that Fairley might kill his son before either shooting himself or climbing out onto the roof and throwing himself to his death. Now and then, the crowd in the streets below, when seeing Fairley at a window, surged backwards fearing the desperate man above might shoot down onto the road.

Someone had gone to fetch Fairley's wife who worked in a nearby mill along with his daughter. The police asked her to go into the building and up the stairs to try and talk her husband into surrendering. This attempt to convince her husband to give himself up was unsuccessful. It became clear that the police were going to have to storm the room and force the issue. The police officers in the forefront using wooden chairs for protection, gathered on the stairway and made their way up the steps. When they got to the top landing the police kicked in the locked front door and they charged the shooter. Fairley was stunned and unable to fire his pistol at the advancing police. In his other hand he held a large knife. The police moved on Fairley, focusing all their attention on the hand holding the gun. During the confusion, Fairley stabbed Inspector McBay in the stomach. The police officer let out a cry of, 'I am stabbed!', but he still held the desperate struggling man.

The police brought the prisoner out into the street, his appearance like something from a horror film. Fairley had received wounds to the head from being hit over the head by police truncheons. The injuries caused a great deal of blood to flow down over the shackled man's face and chest, giving him a hellish appearance. Clothing ripped during the struggle added to his ghastly look. Members of the crowd cried out, 'Lynch him, lynch him!'.

A while later, the injured officer David McBay emerged from the building, brought out on a stretcher. He was sitting up, but a big red stain could be seen, shocking against the white of the bandage. McBay was put in a horse-drawn ambulance van and taken to Dundee Royal Infirmary. Inspector David McBay died from his wounds on 19 August, four days after the stabbing.

Almost immediately questions were asked as to just how this could have happened. On the evening after the tragedy, the *Dundee Evening Telegraph* reported the incident and ran a subheading asking, 'Who was to blame for this outrage?'. The newspaper stated that the police had been aware of Fairley's strange behaviour since 1890, three years before the shooting. People in the area feared Fairley, who was often seen wandering around muttering to himself about the Whitechapel Murders according to the newspaper. It reported at the time that Fairley had a habit of jumping out on passing women crying out, '*Jack the Ripper*'. Fairley was also teased mercilessly by local children who would follow him around crying out, '*Jack the Ripper, Jack the Ripper*'. The troubled man had threatened to shoot his young tormentors and blamed the children's mothers for the abuse.

Fairley had worked as a boiler stoker. He had received a severe blow to his head after an explosion of a boiler in Glasgow. Since then, he had been unable to work and looked after his young son while his wife and fourteen-year-old daughter worked in the mills. Fairley had been to see a doctor in Edinburgh who had passed him fit to work and he was planning to take his family to America to start a new life.

The defence placed a plea of insanity at the High Court in Edinburgh on 10 October 1893. Those doctors brought forward as witnesses all agreed that the prisoner in the dock could not instruct his defence or make a plea owing to his state of mind. The judge agreed and sentenced Fairley to be held at Her Majesty's pleasure.

XIX
Sub-Inspector James Allan
Lanarkshire Constabulary

4 September 1893

It had just gone 11pm on the night of Monday, 4 September 1893, and a young engineer was walking through Bishopbriggs. This man was drunk and making his way to his home in nearby Springburn. The drunk fell at the side of the road near the Crow Tavern and did not get up. In his drunken state it seemed an ideal place to rest and have a wee kip before continuing with his journey. Two men, William Coubrough and Richard McGhee, had found the young man lying unconscious and decided that this was an opportunity too good to miss. They turned out the pockets, stealing ten shillings, tobacco and a clasp knife. The thieves also made off with the drunk man's coat and boots.

At the same time, two police officers, Inspector James Allan and Constable John Pirrie, were told by a railway worker that a drunk man was lying on the road and two men were robbing him. The police officers hurried off in the direction of the crime. The officers met two men walking towards them whereupon they stopped the men and asked if they had seen a man lying in the street. The two told the police officers that they had indeed witnessed a man on the ground. Allan grabbed Coubrough, while Pirrie grabbed McGhee marching them off in the direction of the sleeping man. The inspector and his prisoner were a little in front of Constable Pirrie and his charge. As they made their way up the road, opposite the Crow Tavern, the constable witnessed Coubrough start to struggle with his escort and saw the inspector stagger and fall to the ground, exclaiming, '*I am stabbed!*'.

Allan let go of the man as he fell and Coubrough ran off through adjacent fields and disappeared into the night. Officer Pirrie tried to hand his prisoner over to two young men who were standing at the roadside watching, but they refused to accept responsibility for the prisoner. Pirrie had no option but to escort McGhee to a police station. The prisoner was put into a cell straight away without being searched.

When Pirrie returned, he found Allan lying in a pool of blood. The wounded man had managed to drag himself to the foot of a wall. When Pirrie got to the inspector, he was still alive but only just managed to say, '*I'm dying*', before breathing his last. Inspector James Allan had two stab wounds on his body, a deep one in his groin that was one and a half inches deep and three inches long which had severed an artery. Allan also had a stab wound in his back underneath the shoulder. The police found a blood-stained clasp knife nearby.

While in the cells the police searched McGhee and found the drunk man's stolen clasp knife. When questioned, McGhee told the police that the man responsible for the death of the inspector was William Coubrough. McGhee also stated Coubrough was a ticket-of-leave man (a convict who had a permit to leave prison after serving part of his sentence, with certain restrictions placed on him).

The police wanted Coubrough for failing to report himself (this must have been part of the constraints placed on him). Coubrough had been sentenced on 12 September 1888 at the Glasgow Circuit Court to five-years' penal servitude for breaking into the Broomhill Convalescent Home, Kilsyth. He had served his time in Peterhead Prison from which he was liberated on 17 June 1892.

The Lanarkshire Police Force provided the Glasgow police with a description of the fugitive:

William Coubrough was born in 1854 at Campsie. He is a miner, unmarried, with no fixed residence. He has a shallow complexion, light brown hair, blue eyes, and stands 5ft 5 inches. He has a large number of tattooed marks on his body. These are as follows – ship under sail and figure of a female in fetters on chest: an eagle and flags, a crown and galloping horse on the front of his right forearm; a star, crown, and flags on the outer and back part of his right forearm; a bracelet, harp and anchor on the back of his left wrist; a heart, shamrock, the letters w c h b c o n, on the back of his left hand; a group of flags round a shield and surmounted by a crown on the outer aspect of his right upper arm; a figure on a cross on the outer aspect of his left upper arm; and an anchor on the outer aspect of the left forearm.

Despite a large-scale search involving other police forces, Coubrough seemed to have disappeared. Then on 9 September, a search party of officers from the Lanarkshire and Stirlingshire police forces were searching woods near Campsie. Although the police had scrutinised nearby farm buildings the night before, the superintendent in charge thought they should search them again.

The police officers began searching a farm at Blair Tummoch about four miles north-west of Lennoxtown. While the officers were searching a barn, they found a man asleep in the hay. He was wakened and asked his name. He replied that it was William Coubrough and was arrested. After five days on the run, Coubrough was showing signs of hypothermia and suffering the effects of fatigue. When captured, Coubrough was unaware that Inspector Allan had died. The police took their prisoner to Lennoxtown and from there to Central Police Station, South Albion Street, Glasgow. Locked in a cell known as 'The Cage', two warders watched Coubrough constantly. He was quiet, only asking for food. He was taken to Glasgow's Duke Street Prison to await his trial.

On 30 October 1893, Coubrough was tried at the High Court in Glasgow. The defence argued that the police officer's death was an accident. Coubrough said that he was carrying the knife in his hand and was then collared by Allan. The prisoner said that during the struggle he stabbed the police officer accidentally. The defence argued there was no intent to kill the police officer and the prisoner had suffered great mental agony. Feeling remorse for the death of the police officer, Coubrough's mother had died while he was on the run. Coubrough blamed his mother's death on the worry and shame he had brought her. His defence stated:

The circumstance had affected the mind of the prisoner gravely and he would experience a lasting regret for having caused the deaths of a valued public servant and his mother.

A lesser charge of culpable homicide was accepted. William Coubrough was sentenced to ten-years' penal servitude.

XX
Police Constable Colin MacKenzie
Govan Burgh Police

---

30 August 1896

Police Constable Colin MacKenzie served in the Govan Burgh Police. He was forty-five, when, on 17 August 1896, he was assaulted violently in Quay Park, Govan Road, Govan. The *Glasgow Herald* reported on 1 September that the officer had died from his injuries at the Western Infirmary. The same newspaper said that the police arrested Daniel Hutcheson in connection with the crime; a sailor living at 12 Plantation Street. At the Glasgow Sheriff Court on 25 September 1896, Hutcheson pled not guilty to assault and after hearing two witnesses the Sheriff dismissed the case.

XXI
Police Constable Thomas King
Inverness-shire Constabulary

20 December 1898

Marjory McPherson, known locally as 'Black May', opened the door to the two police constables who stood knocking on the door of her cottage. The two police officers were Thomas King who served at Nethy Bridge and John McNiven based in nearby Boat of Garten. The officers were asking about the whereabouts of Allan MacCallum who had not paid a fine he had received for trespassing. The woman of the house informed the police officer that the man they wanted was not there but was at Loch Garten gathering firewood.

The officers left but they hung around nearby and were surprised to see 'Black May' and her daughter hurriedly leave the house and scurry away. It looked as though the two women were going to warn MacCallum of the police presence in the area around his home. McNiven followed the two women for a while but soon lost them in thick woodland at the back of the cottage. Suddenly, on a high banking above the police officer, MacCallum appeared with a gun pointed at the police constable. The officer knew he was in a hazardous situation. MacCallum was a notorious poacher and known to be an extremely dangerous individual. He threatened to shoot the officer if he took one step forward and then turned around and disappeared into the forest.

Later that afternoon, Constables King and McNiven received information from a young boy that MacCallum was in the cottage. The police officers decided to go and apprehend the wanted man. At about 4pm it was dark and to make matters more difficult for the constables, there was no light on in the house. Having visited it previously, the officers already knew the layout of the cottage and they decided that when they entered, King should go left into the kitchen and McNiven right into the bedroom. As the police officers entered the house, they called out to MacCallum to surrender.

LOCH GARTEN

The two officers walked into the cottage and one went left, the other right. McNiven was stumbling around the bedroom in pitch darkness when suddenly the silence was shattered by a loud gunshot that sounded like it came from outside. McNiven made his way out through the kitchen. In the darkness he was aware of stepping on something soft. When McNiven exited the building, he met a passing postman who informed him that Allan MacCallum had run from the house just after the gunshot. The police officer made his way back into the cottage and this time he took the left door into the kitchen. Lying on the floor in the darkness lay Constable Thomas King; across his legs lay a single-barrel shotgun. McNiven and the postman helped King out from the building, but he died from his wounds before medical help could arrive.

As news of this fatal shooting spread, further police officers were brought from Inverness to hunt for the fugitive. MacCallum was seen running along the road towards Loch Garten without any boots on. The wanted man stopped at a croft and managed to obtain footwear, after which he disappeared into the wilderness.

The police now had a problem. MacCallum was an expert in living off the land as he had been a backwoodsman in America and Australia. MacCallum's father and brother were gamekeepers and he had also been a gamekeeper. MacCallum was a professional poacher who knew every nook and cranny of the area. Rumours that he had managed to climb aboard a slow-moving goods train heading south spread, but Mr MacHardy, the Chief Constable of Inverness, was convinced the fugitive was hiding out in the vicinity.

The police received news that the wanted man had turned up at a lonely croft and had been given oatcakes by the unsuspecting crofter who knew nothing about the killing of the police officer. The crofter told the police that MacCallum had headed east.

On Thursday, 22 December 1898, two days after the shooting, a waxing Moon helped the police search Tomachrocher Farm, the name of which *The Dundee Advertiser* of 24 December 1898 translated into English ironically as Hangman's Knoll. Constable MacBeath, a police officer from Inverness, found MacCallum hiding in a barn. The wanted felon was handcuffed and taken to Aviemore.

Big crowds had assembled to see the prisoner being put onto a train and taken to Inverness Prison. MacCallum who had once been a fit, healthy and strong man now looked dirty and emaciated. The police found a recently sharpened clasp knife on the prisoner.

On 14 February 1899, MacCallum was tried in the Castle of Inverness before Lord Trayner. The Crown accused the prisoner of murdering Constable Thomas King and threatening grievous bodily harm, or attempt to kill, by pointing a loaded gun at Constable John McNiven.

McNiven gave an account of the events on the fateful day of the tragic shooting. Then the postman, Alexander Grant, who saw the gunman escape from the cottage where the shooting took place, took the stand and gave his account. The defence called

CASTLE OF INVERNESS

Donald MacCallum, the prisoner's brother. He stated that his brother had taken ill while in Patagonia, complaining of pains in his head. Donald told the court that the illness his brother contracted overseas had changed him. He added that Allan was quiet at times, and at other times outrageous. Donald explained that his brother had been examined for insanity in 1891. The next witness was an old employer of the prisoner, Mr Graham. He remembered an occasion when the accused had barricaded himself into his house and refused to come out. Graham had written a letter to the Inspector of the Poor stating that he thought MacCallum was insane and dangerous. The defence, running with the possibility that the accused man in the dock was mad, asked the jury, '*Would a man in his ordinary senses for the sake of a five-shilling fine deliberately shoot another man?*'.

The defence argued that in the dark King had been shot by accident. During the judge's summing-up, he said the assertion that Constable King's shooting had been an accident was not supported by the evidence, as the prisoner had never stated before the trial that the shooting was accidental.

The jury retired for twenty minutes. They returned with a verdict of culpable homicide. Lord Trayner told the prisoner that the jury had taken a merciful view and sentenced Allan MacCallum to fifteen-years' penal servitude.

XXII
Police Constable Andrew Urquhart
City of Glasgow Police

24 October 1897

All was quiet in the Queen's Park police office in the early hours of 24 October 1897, when suddenly, just after 4am, a distressed woman burst in through the door. She was a Mrs Battersby who lived in Dixon Avenue. She told the officer at the desk that her son William Mason Battersby, a medical student, was behaving violently at home. Mrs Battersby asked if a police officer could come home with her and try to calm him down. Constable Charles Herriot made his way to the house. The desk sergeant instructed Herriot to get another police officer to accompany him. Herriot blew his whistle on the junction of Allison Street and Cathcart Road and after a couple of sharp blows Constable Andrew Urquhart arrived and joined him.

The three of them made for Dixon Avenue and soon they were at the Battersby's home. When they entered the building, they found William Battersby being held down on the floor in the lobby by family members. The two police officers immediately took charge of the situation, helping William up from the floor as he seemed to have calmed down. As no one in the Battersby family wanted to press charges against young William, and as things seemed to have quietened down, the two constables left the house. The police officers decided to stand out in the road to make sure things stayed peaceful. Almost immediately the officers heard shouting from the house and re-entered the property. William Battersby was holding a poker in the kitchen and threatening to use the weapon on the first person that approached him. Urquhart took hold of a chair to use to defend himself and entered the room. As the police officer attempted to apprehend William, he received blows to the head with the poker. The two officers eventually overpowered the violent man and took him to the station.

As the officers were booking William into the station, Urquhart fell to the floor; he seemed to be having a fit. Doctors Forrest and Clark rushed to the scene as both lived in Dixon Avenue. Unfortunately, Urquhart died before medical help arrived. On examining the police officer's body, no marks except a small scar on his right temple could be found. Urquhart had made no complaint of feeling unwell after being assaulted. Constable Andrew Urquhart hailed from Ross-shire. He was thirty-two and had joined the police force in 1889.

William made his first appearance in court on 25 October. The death of the police officer had gained wide public interest and a large crowd waited outside to see the prisoner taken from the police office to court. Members of the public crammed into the courtroom. Visibly upset, William stood shaking in the dock, crying and nervous. The defence moved to release the prisoner until his trial, arguing that a post-mortem examination showed that the police officer had died from a heart attack. After a minute or so the prisoner returned to the cells. William was then freed until his trial by order of James Hart, the Procurator Fiscal.

The trial of William took place at the Queen's Park police court on 19 November 1897. The defence asked the court to think about:

The great shock the accused must have received by the sudden death at his side of Constable Urquhart on that Sunday morning, and the mental agony which he had endured since then, but especially immediately after the occurrence.

The defence suggested a fine would have been a proper punishment for William. The Baillie did not think a fine was a sufficient sentence and instead ordered William Battersby to thirty-days' imprisonment. At this, the young medical student shouted, *'Give me another month and be done with it'*. He was escorted from the court by two constables.

XXIII
Police Constable James Harte
Leith Burgh Police

4 April 1900

Labourer Henry Millar was making a nuisance of himself on the night of 2 April 1900. Millar was drunk and noisily staggered along Newhaven Road in the Leith area of Edinburgh.

Two officers, Police Constables Harte and McDonald, who were sent to apprehend Millar on a charge of breach of the peace, tried to arrest the drunk man who resisted violently. Millar kicked both constables on the legs, and during the struggle, Harte received a savage kick to his abdomen whereupon he staggered and fell to the ground. McDonald managed to get his struggling colleague to the Newhaven Police Station. Inside the police building the officer collapsed. The injured police officer was taken home to Prince Regent Street; he never regained consciousness. He died on 4 April 1900. James Harte was thirty-eight and, having been married twice, left a large family of eight behind.

A post-mortem showed that Constable James Harte had died of natural causes. Consequently, James Millar was only charged and found guilty of assault.

XXIV
Police Constable William George MacKelvie
Hawick Burgh Police

20 July 1906

On the evening of Saturday, 14 July 1906, the pubs in the border town of Hawick were full of drinkers. The *Edinburgh Evening News* described Hawick that night as full with a somewhat disorderly crowd. Later, tragedy would shock the border town as news spread that a police officer was savagely beaten while going about his duty and lay in a critical state.

Frank MacCulloch, a hawker, spent the day drinking in the inns of Hawick. Come nightfall he was extremely drunk and making a bit of a nuisance of himself. Two police officers approached the drunk MacCulloch as he and a friend walked from the Howegate to the High Street. After an altercation, the officers grabbed the intoxicated men. During the struggle Frank attacked Constable William George MacKelvie. The drunk man and the police officer fought, and both fell to the ground. MacCulloch punched and kicked out at the officer as the two of them rolled around in the street.

MacCulloch was eventually arrested and taken to a police station while MacKelvie continued with his duties. When his shift had ended, and he had gone home, MacKelvie felt a severe pain in his stomach. As a result of internal injuries received while arresting MacCulloch, MacKelvie died.

MacCulloch was arrested and tried for murder on 30 August 1906. His defence counsel pled not guilty to a charge of murder but guilty to a reduced charge of culpable homicide. The defence argued that the injuries on the police officer were not intentional and happened while the prisoner resisted arrest. MacCulloch showed real remorse following the MacKelvie's death; he had not been in trouble before.

The court accepted the lesser plea. The judge told the accused that his utter recklessness as to the effect the assault would have was near murder in the eye of the law before passing a sentence of seven-years' penal servitude. As MacCulloch left the court he shouted towards the public gallery, 'Keep your hearts up!'.

XXV
Police Constable James Campbell
City of Glasgow Police

20 January 1919

On the night of 20 January 1919, Constable James Campbell was out on patrol in Glasgow. At around midnight, Campbell entered the backcourt of 637 Great Eastern Road. In the backcourt, the police officer surprised a man dressed in dark clothing who was acting suspiciously at the back premises of a jeweller's shop. The officer went to apprehend the man.

As the police officer approached, the man drew out a pistol and shot the officer twice. One bullet hit Campbell on the left side of his neck and the other entered his stomach. He collapsed and the shooter disappeared. The noise of the shots and a weak cry of help brought people in the tenements out to investigate where they found Campbell lying face-down in a pool of blood.

At Glasgow Royal Infirmary the gravely wounded officer was able to describe the man who shot him:

> [A] young man between 19 and 21 years old. . . 5 feet 6 or 7 inches, of dark build, clean-shaven, and dressed in dark clothing, including a muffler and grey cap.

Campbell never recovered, succumbing to his injuries. The police picked up several people in connection with this shooting but charged no one.

XXVI
Police Constable William McGregor
City of Glasgow Police

1 June 1920

On 31 January 1919, the First World War had been over for nearly three months and soldiers returning home had not found the 'Land fit for Heroes' promised to them by Prime Minister Lloyd George. Unemployment and poor overcrowded housing were the welcome those returning home received.

To combat high-level unemployment, trade unions wanted a reduction in the working week from the wartime level of 54 hours to 40 hours, hoping that this decrease would create more jobs.

The Clyde Workers Committee (CWC) called a strike on 27 January. Two days later, they handed in their demands to the Provost of Glasgow to convey to the government. On 31 January at 10.30am a delegation of the CWC turned up at the City Chambers to receive the government's answer to the demands. The union leaders, including William Gallagher and David Kirkwood, were shown into a waiting area as the Provost was in a meeting with the shipyard owners. Crowds of thousands consisting of strikers and unemployed men flooded into George Square.

If the government failed to meet their demands, the union leaders threatened to stop the trams running, the electricity from flowing and effectively shut down the city. The striking workers targeted the trams in George Square. A large crowd gathered around one tram in the square and stopped it.

A young soldier in khaki uniform jumped on the rear platform and shouted at the strikers to let the tram through. The crowd around the tram continued to prevent it from moving. The police moved in to protect the vehicle forming a cordon around the stranded trolleybus. The strikers surged forward as the police drew their batons to drive the crowd back. Fighting broke out and missiles rained down on the police. Mounted police emerged from the quadrangle within the City Chambers and a full-scale battle broke out in front of the council buildings.

Kirkwood ran out of the City Chambers to try and pacify the crowd. A blow from a police baton promptly felled him. Meanwhile, Gallagher who was addressing the masses, was arrested. While all this mayhem was taking place thousands more flocked into the square led by a brass band. The police tried to break up the group. This police action resulted in widespread fighting. The authorities decided to read the Riot Act so the Lord Provost along with the Sheriff Principal, the Chief Constable and the Town Clerk left the City Chambers to read aloud the Act, meaning by law the assembled protestors would have to disperse.

The strikers had looted a lorry loaded with empty bottles. As the officials tried to read the Act, the Sheriff had it ripped from his hands and bottles rained down. While the Sheriff recited the Act from memory, a bottle hit his hand, and another hit the Chief Constable in the face. The Sheriff completed the reading of the Riot Act and

GEORGE SQUARE AND GLASGOW CITY CHAMBERS

the officials withdrew to the safety of the City Chambers.

The police escorted Kirkwood and Gallagher into the City Chambers and they were given permission to address the crowd from the balcony. The union leaders pleaded with the multitude to disperse from George Square and make their way to Glasgow Green. This plea was accepted and the protestors, led by the brass band, started to make its way towards the Green. At Glasgow Cross more trouble erupted and tram cars were attacked. Missiles were hurled through tram windows as the passengers inside fled. The strikers climbed on to the top of the trams and pulled the trolley pole which connects the tram to the overhead electric lines. The poles were bent and twisted, thus making them useless, so by the time the police had driven the crowd from Glasgow Cross, a dozen trams lay destroyed.

By the end of the day, thirty-four civilians and nineteen police officers had sustained injuries. Fearing further disturbances and the threat of this unrest becoming a political revolution, the government mindful of the recent revolution in Russia, poured troops into Glasgow. Thousands of soldiers and six tanks marched upon the city and the military placed machine-gun nests on the top of the City Chambers and the buildings around George Square. The troops in Glasgow's Maryhill Barracks were confined to their quarters as the establishment feared that if serious trouble flared up, the Glasgow based forces might join with their fellow citizens. Two sentries stopped anyone visiting the City Chambers; at the main door, the soldiers wore steel helmets and had rifles with fixed bayonets.

As darkness fell a problem in the electric supply left the centre of Glasgow in semi-darkness. This lack of street lighting allowed opportunists to take advantage of the situation by smashing windows and looting shops.

GLASGOW GREEN AND THE PEOPLE'S PALACE

Amongst those injured during the disturbances was Police Constable William McGregor. He received a hit on the head with a bottle. McGregor was from Nairnshire and was twenty-six. McGregor had served with the Scots Guards throughout the war. After being injured he seemed to recover and went back to work at the end of February 1920; he only worked for a day or two before having to give it up again. The officer died on 1 June. The authorities reported that his death resulted from a blow to the head received during the night of 31 January.

This account of the cause of the police officer's death was hotly disputed. The Socialist newspaper *Forward* argued that McGregor's death was due to heart disease and pneumonia. The paper quoted a letter from a patient in Ward 33 of Glasgow Infirmary which stated:

> *At no time from 9 April to his death on 1 June was he under surgical treatment for injuries. His case all the while was regarded as medical and treated as such. He may have been suffering from cardiac trouble for several years.*

The paper also detailed that McGregor would not have been allowed back to work unless the medical advisers of the police department thought him fully recovered.

A day or two after the events of 31 January, the Lord Provost of Glasgow made a remarkable speech to a group of ex-prisoners of war. Referring to the strikers, the Provost stated:

> *I am struggling to find an excuse for such conduct. My colleagues and I realise that these men have been labouring under prolonged physical strain for such a time that possibly it may have affected their nervous system. I hope that with some patience their mental balance may be restored. Conduct such as we have had makes one despair that they have any mental balance or are ever likely to have it.*

The Provost's statement is shocking. It shows a complete lack of any understanding of the social conditions and genuine concerns of the working class at the time.

XXVII
Police Inspector Robert Johnston
City of Glasgow Police

4 May 1921

On the morning of 4 May 1921, witnesses noticed small groups of men hanging about Glasgow's High Street. John Smith, an electrical engineer, who had his premises at the corner of Burrell's Lane and the High Street, noticed two men standing across the road at 10.15am. He watched one of the men walk down the street and go into a bakery. The man came out of the shop eating a cake. He walked back to his companion and offered him one. The man waved to two men standing at the other side of the street and they too were each given a cake.

Just after midday, tram motorman George McCracken was walking down the High Street past Cathedral Square when he noticed what he was to describe as an unusual number of men loitering about between Rotten Row and Duke Street. McCracken thought this so strange that he stopped a police officer, Constable Grant, and pointed it out to him.

Things were not right in Glasgow that day. A taxi firm received a call from Mary Tracey employed at undertakers Tracey of Parkhead. The woman asked for a taxi to pick up a Mr Mitchell from the Ivanhoe Hotel in Buchanan Street. Alexander McKechnie, the taxi driver, picked up Mitchell and took him as requested to 74 Abercromby Street. Mitchell went into the close and returned alone and the taxi took him back to the hotel. After waiting outside for half an hour, Mitchell left the hotel once more. The taxi took Mitchell back to the address in Abercromby Street. This time Mitchell returned to the vehicle with a second man and the taxi was asked to go to Cathedral Square. There, both men left the cab and returned a short while later and asked to be taken back to Abercromby Street. Mitchell went into St Mary's Chapel, leaving his companion in the car. Mitchell came from the church and asked to be taken to McLeod Street. When they arrived, both men got out of the car and walked in the direction of

Cathedral Square. After waiting for half an hour, Mitchell returned with a different man. The passengers told the driver to go to Dale Street (now Tradestone Street) and once there, the other man got out the car and walked towards Clyde Place. He was gone about ten minutes. When the man returned, he was carrying a long thin package wrapped in brown paper which he was trying to hide under his overcoat. The taxi driver thought it looked like a rifle. The taxi drove the passengers to 8 McLeod Street. The men left the car, telling the driver to wait. He waited for two hours but the men did not return.

At about 12.25pm, a police van was travelling up the High Street, delivering prisoners from the police office to Duke Street Prison. The van slowed down to turn into the Drygate (now Cathedral Square, opposite the Barony Hall) and as it slowed the driver changed down gears. Inside the front of the van were the driver, Constable Ross, Detective-Sergeant George Stirton and two other police officers – Detective MacDonald and Inspector Robert Johnston. Two police constables – David Brown and George Bernard – were in the rear compartment of the van guarding a prisoner convicted of indecent assault. Two of the police officers were armed. In the other compartment just behind the driver was IRA man Frank Carty.* The police had arrested him on 28 April when they discovered him hiding out at 89 Barlogan Avenue, Glasgow. Carty was wanted for breaking out of Sligo Jail.

As the van slowed, shots rang out. Bullets hit the radiator, stopping the vehicle. A gun battle erupted in the street around the van. Stirton and Johnston fired back at the gunmen who were firing from all directions. Johnston was hit in the chest and fell out onto the road fatally injured, while Stirton was shot in the wrist. A couple of the attackers tried to force open the rear door of the police vehicle but were not able to break the lock, so they fired their revolvers through the keyholes, forcing the three men inside to lie on the floor.

---

* Frank Carty was a senior figure in the IRA during the Irish War of Independence of 1919–21.

DUKE STREET PRISON, GLASGOW

As all this was going on the driver, Ross, managed to restart the van. The police escort took off towards the safety of the nearby prison. All the gunmen fled the scene. Although injured, Stirton chased the attackers – who numbered ten men – along the Rotten Row until he was unable to run any more. A woman who lived locally and had been a nurse came out and tended to the wounded officer's arm.

A party of gunmen were spotted running along the Drygate holding revolvers in their raised hands. The men made their way to the High Street, put their guns into their pockets and disappeared into the crowds.

The police dragnet saw over thirty people arrested in connection with this attack. These included a woman and a priest. On 9 August 1921, thirteen men were tried at the High Court in Edinburgh. They were Daniel Patrick Walsh alias Joseph Dunn alias James Mitchell, Daniel Branniss alias Charles Grier, James McCarra, John McGarrigle, Vincent Campbell, John Carney, William Fullerton, James Fullerton, Michael O'Carroll, Sean O'Daire, James Kavanagh, Thomas Tracey and Francis O'Hagen.

All the accused pled not guilty to charges:

[Of] having conspired with other people to further the objects of Sinn Fein by the unlawful use of force and violence and especially by means of explosives, firearms, &c., to the danger of the lives and persons and property of the lieges; of having conspired to release from the custody of the police authorities Frank Carty alias Frank Somers, a member of the Irish Republican Army who had been arrested on charges of theft and prison-breaking in Ireland, by breaking into the police patrol van in which he was being conveyed to the Duke Street Prison on 4 May 1921; of having assembled, armed and loaded firearms and discharged these at certain police officers and murdered Inspector Johnston and seriously injured Detective Stirton to the danger of his life: or alternatively to the later part of the charge of having assembled in High Street and discharged firearms at four police officers and murdered Inspector Johnston and destroyed the lock of the police patrol van and attempted to force it open.

On the morning of 9 May, the Crown called witnesses to give evidence regarding the suspicious behaviour of the men seen milling around the High Street. When the taxi driver, Alexander McKechnie, testified, he told the court that he had picked out his passenger when shown several men in the Duke Street Prison. The driver admitted he recognised the man in the prison yard, but only after a cap, like the one worn by Mitchell on 4 May was put on the suspect's head – the prisoner also had his glasses removed. McKechnie also picked out Tracey when asked to choose anyone he recognised in Glasgow's Central Police Station. The taxi driver failed to identify any of the other men who got into his taxi that morning. John Smith, who watched the men acting strangely and sharing cakes from his shop, could not pick out anyone when shown suspects. A Mrs Grant pointed to one man she saw acting strangely as being McCarra.

Several police officers who were on duty in the area on the morning picked out Carney, Kavanagh, Tracey, McCarra and both William and James Fullerton as the men huddling in groups on the morning of the attempted bust out. Constable Grant, who had received a warning about the strange men, picked out McCarra, although when cross-examined admitted that on the morning in question he did not see the man's face or features as he had his back to him.

The court called witnesses who saw the attack or were in the area just afterwards to testify next. Some told the court that they had seen O'Hagen, Michell and James Fullerton in the area after the attack. The next witness was Detective Stirton and after giving an account of the events that morning, he told the court that when he got out of hospital, he was taken to the Duke Street Prison. In prison, he identified Mitchell, Grier, McCarra, McGarrigle, Carney, William Fullerton, O'Carroll, O'Daire and Kavanagh as the men involved in the gun battle. Stirton told the court that Mitchell was one of the men at the rear of the police vehicle trying to force open the doors. The detective talked of seeing McCarra, Grier, O'Daire and William Fullarton standing in the street holding their revolvers in their right hand but resting the guns on their extended left arm to give them more stability while shooting at the van.

One of the defence lawyers, Mr Sandeman, pointed out that Stirton had managed to pick out nine men while he was only allowed to see them in prison for a couple of minutes. Then came a remarkable accusation by Vincent Campbell's lawyer, Morrice Mackay KC, who accused Stirton of firing the first shot. The police officer denied this accusation and then the lawyer charged the police, not used to carrying firearms, of being overcome with fear. Stirton replied, '*I don't think the Glasgow police are so frightened as to be overcome by fear*'. This accusation is incredible given the bravery shown by all the police officers ambushed that day, not to mention George Stirton who, while injured and having dropped his revolver, still chased a group of armed and extremely dangerous men along the Rotten Row.

The next day in court the damage to the police vehicle was described. It had a bullet hole in the front window, three bullets had hit the radiator, a bullet had severed the tube to the horn and there were bullet holes below the driver's seat, with another just above the driver's head. The lock at the rear of the van had a bullet in it. Detective-Constable McDonald, who had been sitting next to the driver, told of seeing three men approach the van. At this time, Stirton got out of his seat and said, '*Here they come!*', indicating that the police were expecting an attempted rescue. McDonald then told of firing his Webley Revolver at the gunmen and identified O'Carroll, Grier, McCarra, Campbell, William Fullarton and O'Daire as the men the police officer was shooting at during the battle. McDonald admitted that it was impossible to say who shot Inspector Johnston.

Sandeman went on to quiz the officer about the action taken by the police that day. Establishing that the first few shots fired by the police were from inside the front of the van, this was the police returning fire and were shot through the front window. Sandeman thought firing back through the glass was silly. McDonald replied, '*You don't wait to be shot. I did not think the glass would deflect the shots*'.

There was a lighter discussion when McDonald was asked by one of the defence lawyers, Mr MacKay, why he had not shot the guns out of the hands of the people attacking him. The officer answered that that was hard to do. Mackay admitted that he had been watching too many films, to which the judge stated regarding Hollywood, '*They never miss*'.

Asked about his ability to recognise the men shooting at him, the officer stated that he was confident the men he had pointed out were the ones shooting that morning. The defence put to McDonald that before the trial he told colleagues he could only identify one man. The police officer denied this. In addition, the driver Constable Ross had his ability to positively identify the attackers questioned. The officer denied being taken into the cell of O'Daire on the evening of 4 May and failing to recognise him, only to change his mind and point out O'Daire as one of the IRA men.

A police witness discussed the day of O'Hagan's arrest at a house in 69 Abbotsford Place. He stated that when the police arrived O'Hagan noted there was no person in Glasgow tonight sorrier than he was for the death of the inspector. When asked outright by the witness if he was a member of Sinn Fein, O'Hagan stated that he was. The police officer admitted that when they arrested O'Hagan, he seemed sincerely sorry about the death of Inspector Johnston and seemed anxious to make it clear that he had nothing to do with the murder.

Then Tracey was questioned regarding his involvement and asked about the phone call to the taxi firm instructing them to send a car to the Ivanhoe Hotel and the tab for this to be put on Tracey's business account. Initially both Traceys were charged with being involved in the attack, but Mrs Tracey was later released. Mr Tracey told the court that a man had come into their office just before 8am on 4 May and asked for a car to be sent to the hotel to pick up a man called Mitchell. Tracey stated he had not seen this man before and did not know him. Tracey denied any knowledge when questioned about a letter the police found in his shop addressed to a Kate Lee. This letter was addressed to the wife of a Thomas Lee of 70 Tod Street, Parkhead, Glasgow, who had been convicted months previously when police stopped a suspicious car in Alloa. The police found a large quantity of ammunition and explosives in the vehicle.

The next witness called was John Glaister MD, Professor of Forensic Medicine at the University of Glasgow. Glaister went on to talk about the post-mortem he conducted on the dead police officer. The doctor stated the cause of death was a bullet which entered Johnston's left breast. It passed through the left chamber of the heart, the liver and stomach before lodging in the dead man's spine.

Then Alexander Drummond Drysdale, the governor of Duke Street Prison was called. Drysdale gave an account of the procedure used in identifying the men held in connection with the shooting of Johnston. He told the court that the persons asked to pick out those involved had to look out of a small window overlooking a yard. The governor stated that he allowed only one person at the window at a time. The prisoners paraded past this window. The observer looking at the suspects got a clear view of the side and the full face of the men in the yard as they passed. Drysdale said that Stirton identified nine of the accused this way. Stirton pointed out the men he thought had taken part in the attack and a Lieutenant McDonald noted their names. Drysdale considered this so important to get right that Stirton then went outside into the yard and again picked out the men. When asked if the officer was in any way tutored as to the men to select, the governor replied, 'Not at the prison'.

The following day was 12 August, and the governor of the prison was again called to take the stand. He was asked once more about the identification of Mitchell by Detective Stirton. The defence asked the question about placing the cap on the suspect's head and removing the man's glasses. The defence thought it wrong that someone should alter the dress of one of the prisoners in the presence of someone asked to conduct an identification. The governor stated that the prisoner should parade in the clothing he was wearing when brought into the prison. Asked if McDonald and Stirton had conversed with one another during the identification parade, the governor accepted that they might have. The prison official stated he did not hear what they were discussing. Asked why he had previously said that the police officers did not talk, the governor admitted that when he heard them converse, he did not stop them. The prison official stated if he had heard them talking about the prisoners under surveillance, he would have prevented the officers from discussing the suspects. The lawyer then asked the governor what he thought about the fact that one police officer identified nine men after observing them for only two minutes and another police officer was able to pick out eight. The witness admitted that he thought it remarkable, and when asked, if in his experience, he had known anything comparable with it, the governor answered, 'I don't think so'. When asked if when the prisoners were paraded around the yard, did they stop in front of the men at the window, the prison official answered that he did not think so. He admitted that there was so short a time and stated that the identification process was conducted smartly.

John Daniel Whitehead and Thomas Henry, both warders at

Strangeways Prison, Manchester, took the stand. The two men stated that they knew James Mitchell as Daniel Patrick Walsh who had escaped from Strangeways on 25 October 1919.

The next witness, Detective Louis Noble, Central Division of the Glasgow Police, was asked how many people the police had brought in to identify the accused, Noble replied, *'About a hundred'*. The police officer admitted that apart from witnesses who were serving police officers, the civilian witnesses recognised few of the men. Noble stated that civilians only identified one or two suspects. In contrast, the police officers were able to point out eight or nine.

Things took a turn on 15 August when the Crown dismissed the case against Francis O'Hagan as his mental state had deteriorated in prison. Dr James Harvey, Acting Medical Officer, HM Prison Edinburgh, was called and stated O'Hagan was not fit to stand trial.

The trial continued with information disclosed about an arms cache being discovered by the police in a cellar at 74 Abercromby Street. Following a tip-off, the authorities decided to keep watch on the address. The police searched cellars around the property. The first search on 30 June, weeks after the IRA attack, revealed a rifle along with painting equipment. During a further search police unearthed:

12 Colt automatic pistols, 3 German automatic pistols, 8 Mauser pistols, 3 Webley revolvers, 3 Smith & Wesson revolvers, six small revolvers, 955 rounds of rifle, revolver and pistol ammunition, one pouch and four holsters, two magazines, a magazine filler, a bayonet, a coil of fuse, eight boxes of percussion caps, 21 packets of gelignite, case containing 14 detonators, 82 detonators and a length of wire, six hand grenades, a bomb and a torch.

James Porter of 74 Abercromby Street was arrested but later released after denying any knowledge of the arms. He was not in the habit of using the unlocked basement.

The Crown called Mary Tracey. She had been a suspect and had been held in custody for over 11 weeks before being released. Tracey stated that her husband, Thomas, had never been a member of Sinn Fein or the IRA. She told the court that a young man had come into the office to book a taxi, backing up her husband's earlier account. She also gave her husband Thomas an alibi. Mrs Tracey told the court that at the time of the shooting her husband and his friend, James Brennan, were at a house in Shettleston making the arrangements for a funeral. Mrs Tracey stated that Thomas returned at 12.30pm and went back out to attend a funeral at 3.30pm. She said that when Thomas returned, she noticed no trace of anxiety.

James Brennan, a steel smelter, sometimes helped the funeral director and he backed up Mary Tracey's account of her husband's movements on the morning of the attack. Other witnesses stated that Tracey was at Shettleston on the morning of 4 May. A barber, William Craig, said that at the time of the IRA attack Tracey had come into his shop for a shave. Another witness stated that they saw the accused at the front door of his shop at 12.40pm on 4 May.

Then the mother of Michael O'Carroll stated that Michael was in bed until noon on 4 May. She said that her unemployed son was in the habit of sleeping late. He left the house at around 1.30pm to go to the Labour Club. Mrs O'Carroll did admit that both she and her son were members of a Sinn Fein club. John Troy, a ship painter, told the court of being in the O'Carroll's house on the morning of 4 May, and seeing the prisoner in the dock in the house until 12.30pm.

More witnesses gave alibis for John Carney, a barber who had a shop in Govan Road. One witness stated that he had his hair cut by the accused at the time of the gun battle. Another witness, Louis Carroll, noted that Sean O'Daire had dinner with him and his mother at Possilpark at 1pm on the day of the attempted heist. Another witness stated that during the afternoon he had accompanied O'Daire and Carney to the home of fellow-accused, William and James Fullerton, to borrow a bicycle.

Mrs Mary Lavin gave James Mitchell an alibi. Mitchell's landlady, Mrs Lavin, stated that the accused had been lodging with her at

173 Thomson Street. On the morning of 4 May, Mitchell sat reading the paper until he left the house at 12.15pm. Next, Thomas Ryan, a superintendent of the Irish National Insurance Company, told the court that he had met Mitchell in Thomson Street at 12.15pm and together they went to visit the doctor as Mitchell felt unwell. As the doctor was not in, the two men went into town and had lunch together. A girl employed at the doctor's remembered seeing Ryan around the time and confirmed his testimony. The girl said that as she spoke to Ryan, she noticed another man who had stayed outside. Asked to identify the man at the doctor's, the girl looked at the accused and said she thought it was the man in the dock, James Mitchell. A man who owned a shop in Great Eastern Road, near the doctor's, also stated that he saw Mitchell on the day and time stated.

The next day more witnesses were brought out to give the accused men alibis. George Butchart, a newsagent, stated that he saw John McGarrigle at 33 Hope Street during the time of the offence. Daniel Harrigan backed this up as he also saw the accused on the morning around the time of the attack. In the witness stand, McGarrigle explained that he had been in the army during the First World War. He told the court he had served in Egypt, Palestine, Gallipoli and Germany. He went on to recount how during the war he had been wounded in the shoulder and that the bullet found by the police was that with which he had been shot and kept by him as a souvenir. The prisoner denied being anywhere near the alleged offence, giving the names of people who could vouch for him. He also told of his shock when the police raided the house he was visiting at 74 Abercromby Street. The address was the home of Vincent Campbell. The witness was there with several of his fellow accused on the evening of 4 May. He told of his surprise when a police officer found a revolver in the room. When cross-examined McGarrigle stated that in all the time he had been in the building, he had never seen a gun. The accused also denied being a member of the IRA.

The Solicitor-General, C D Murray, KC, MP, reminded the court that being a member of Sinn Fein was not illegal, but being involved in furthering the aims of the Irish Republican group using violent means, was. The Solicitor-General also stated that it did not matter who shot the police officer dead as you were equally guilty if you shot at the police or the police vehicle. Murray noted that the men did not have to have been there attacking the police to be guilty. The Crown established that if the accused took an active part in the planning of the attack it would result in a conviction.

Then the lawyers for the defence stood before the jury. The first was Sandeman. He called the Glasgow police cocksure. Sandeman, again referring to the City Police Force said mockingly, *'Be bold, be alert, be cocksure'.* The lawyer went on to say in a condescending way, *'Surely no bolder set of men existed than those in the Glasgow Police Force'.* A few people in the public gallery started to applaud but the court officials put a stop to this show of support. Sandeman also pointed out that while over one hundred people tried to identify the prisoners in the dock as the men involved, only three people could positively point out anyone for sure.

The next day was 19 August and Mackey speaking for the seven men he was defending against the charge of murder, questioned the accusation of plotting to murder. The lawyer stated that the men shooting at the police van that morning were initially only trying to stop the vehicle and force open the locked back doors. It was only after the police fired at them that they returned fire. The council for the defence then stated that on the morning of 4 May, Detective Stirton was wired. Mackey noted that when the gunman stepped out from the shadows Stirton was a man all on wires. He jumped up excitedly, shouting out, *'Here they are'*, shot through the glass screen, jumped down and took deliberate aim at a man. Mackey also said that all the accused men could provide the most convincing and unshaken proof that they were not there. Mackey spoke of the evidence against James Mitchell which he called far from satisfactory and certainly not sufficient to warrant a verdict of murder. Mackey told the jury that they did not have enough evidence to convict any of the accused.

On 20 August 1921, the jury returned after an absence of an hour and a half and declared the charges against James Mitchell, Charles Grier, James McCarra, Vincent Campbell and John Carney not proven. The remaining accused, John McGarrigle, James Fullerton, Michael O'Carroll, Sean O'Daire, James Kavanagh and Thomas Tracey were found not guilty. All were released. James Mitchell was subsequently rearrested for escaping from Strangeways Prison in England.

In our modern times of high-tech surveillance, it seems incredible that around a dozen men should stand in a city high street, engage in a gun battle with the police resulting in an officer being shot dead and another severely wounded and not one man is convicted of the crime. The police initially arrested thirty-eight people and took statements from over a hundred witnesses but could not positively connect any of the suspects with the crime. The main problem for the prosecution was that these men all produced perfect alibis. People came forward to state that they were with or had seen the accused men in areas away from the crime at the time the van attack was taking place. Were these witnesses, living in a city and indeed an area of Scotland where people were sympathetic to the Irish Republican cause, simply giving the men alibis out of sympathy or duty to a common goal? Did the IRA members who undertook the attack have a sophisticated system to make sure these men, if caught, would not be hanged, making use of large numbers of friends or Sinn Fein sympathisers with prearranged statements giving the accused men an alibi? Or were the police, desperate to find the men responsible for the murder of one of their own, too enthusiastic in rounding up any Sinn Fein member that fitted the age and description of the men involved in the crime? The Crown admitted during the trial that being a member of Sinn Fein was not illegal. We may never know the answers to this fascinating story.

XXVIII
Police Constable Peter Hunter Munro
Lanarkshire Constabulary

7 August 1921

During the evening of 5 August 1921, a large crowd walked into Wishaw after watching a schoolchildren's football match at Newmains. A flute band headed the group which numbered around two hundred people. People in the crowd started to hurl abuse at a couple of police officers near the Wishaw Cross. Cries of '*Up Dublin!*' and other Irish Republican slogans filled the air. The police became the object of other threatening and derogatory abuse.

Two police officers, Constables Peter Munro and George Davidson, moved in to arrest the ringleaders. Munro grabbed hold of one man, but members of the crowd attacked the officer, punching and kicking him. Munro fell to the ground and the assault continued. Other police officers ran to assist, and a general mêlée erupted. Constable Stewart grabbed hold of one of the men seen attacking the police. The man struggled free and ran into the YMCA building. The officer dragged the man out and after a violent struggle hauled him onto a tram car. Other officers with batons in hand helped Munro to his feet, but he collapsed once again. Constable Peter Munro died two days later in the Glasgow Royal Infirmary from his injuries.

On 26 October 1921, Edward Higgins, Peter Grady, Frank Cornin, George Reddington, James Donnelly, James Mulhern, John Grady, James Hastie and William Hastie all stood before a judge accused of assault and murder. All denied the charges.

During the trial, nineteen-year-old Constable Davidson gave an account of the disturbance on 5 August. He told of seeing a flute band approach and of watching Munro grapple with Edward Higgins, one of the accused. Davidson spoke of seeing Higgins strike Constable Munro once on the jaw and once on the face. The next witness was Stewart who stated that he saw Peter Grady strike Munro. Stewart talked of being involved in a struggle with Grady who resisted violently when arrested.

Asked by the judge about the shouts of Up Dublin! and whether this was a political cry or hooligans' cry, Stewart replied that the population often shouted this at the police in the area. Officer Alex McLean, in response to this question, stated that the cry was often used for the fun of it.

When called to give evidence, Peter Grady told of being at a school football match and returning from Newmains but denied that the crowd was riotous. Grady said that he saw a man being arrested and went to see what was happening. The accused then stated a blow from a police baton felled him. Grady spoke of being dragged up by the police and one officer holding his arms behind his back while another hit him with his truncheon, but the witness denied hitting Munro. Another of the accused men, Frank Cornin, stated, '*The police seem to think I am a Sinn Feiner and associated with the Sinn Fein organisation. I wish to make it clear that I am not associated with them*'.

William Hastie had a strong alibi so the Crown withdrew the case against him. The jury found Edward Higgins guilty of culpable homicide and sentenced him to five-years' penal servitude. Peter Grady and John Grady were found guilty of mobbing and rioting and assault upon the police and received sentences of twelve- and six-months' imprisonment (respectively). George Reddington and James Donnelly were each handed four-month terms. James Mulhern and Frank Cornin were both found not guilty.

XXIX
Assistant Chief Constable Robert Chisholm Thomson
Edinburgh City Police

18 July 1940

Alexander John MacPherson, an RAF sergeant, sat in the pub with his friends on the evening of 12 July 1940. Stationed in England as a gun instructor and on leave back home for forty-eight hours, the

RAF man drank four half pints of beer and had two nips of whisky before leaving the public house with two bottles of beer and heading home to 9 Northfield Broadway, Edinburgh.

Later that night, the air raid siren woke MacPherson. After taking his family to the safety of the shelter, he grabbed his rifle and stopped a car travelling along the road. He told the driver, John Walker, that the streets were to be kept clear during an air raid for emergency vehicles, despite this being an Auxiliary Fire Service (AFS) car. Walker would later state that the RAF man smelled of drink.

After letting the AFS car continue with a stern warning, MacPherson noticed a light that he initially thought was a small fire. He saw that it was car headlights approaching him. The soldier, with his rifle in his hand, shouted, '*Halt!*' at the car he thought was travelling far too fast.

MacPherson believed that the vehicle showed no signs of slowing down and again shouted a warning, '*Halt, or I fire!*'. The car passed the RAF sergeant. MacPherson levelled his rifle and took a shot at the vehicle as it headed down the road, trying to hit the rear tyre and force it off the highway.

The car driver, Constable Robert Bruce Knox, saw a dark figure at the side of the road on the right. Suddenly his windscreen shattered and his passenger, Assistant Chief Constable Robert Chisholm Thomson, lunged forward and groaned, '*They have shot me*'.

The police car came to a screeching halt. Constable Thompson who was sitting in the back jumped out and shouted at the figure standing by the side of the road, '*You have shot the Assistant Chief Constable of Edinburgh!*''. The RAF man refused to go to the police station stating, that as a member of the military, the police were not authorised to arrest him.

At his trial at the High Court in Edinburgh on 17 September 1940, Sergeant MacPherson was adamant that he had not committed a crime and was only doing his duty and following orders. As far as the RAF man was concerned, he had set up a roadblock and if a car failed to stop, he was entitled to fire at the vehicle. MacPherson stated this was a direct order from his wing commander.

Police Constable Harold Smith who had been in the car that night, denied hearing an order to halt. When the judge asked Smith, *'Did you see any movement such as a person would make to attract the attention of the car?'*, Smith replied, *'I did not'* and when asked about hearing a shout, the police officer replied that he heard, *'No shout whatsoever'.*

James Manson, an Air Raid Precautions (ARP) Warden, contradicted Smith's testimony stating that he heard a shout of halt, followed by a shot. To add to the confusion, another ARP Warden, Robert Laird Graham, told the court he heard a shot first and then a shout. The defence later brought in more witnesses who claimed to have listened to a distinctive shout. Peter Ross Jefferies, an architect, told the court he heard three distinct challenges and then a shot. George Nisbet said that he heard a shout of stop that car then halt being shouted twice before he heard a rifle shot. A Mrs Brierley stated she heard, halt twice, and halt or I fire before a shot.

John Walker, the auxiliary firefighter who was stopped by MacPherson before the police car incident, gave evidence to the court. Walker told of being flagged down and of MacPherson pointing his rifle at him and telling him to put his hands up. The RAF soldier told Walker to shut his mouth. Walker stated that at the time he thought MacPherson was under the influence of drink.

Norman Duncan, who drank with the accused in the pub on the night of 12 July stated that he did not consider MacPherson to have been drunk or showing the effects of drink. Dr James Deuchars who examined MacPherson in the police station after his arrest said that he was not under the influence of drink to such an extent as to be incapable of the control of his faculties.

Flight Lieutenant William Thomas Doherty stated that the man in the dock was efficient, conscientious and keen. When asked, Duncan admitted that MacPherson was also impulsive and a strict disciplinarian.

On 18 July, MacPherson was called to the stand to give evidence. The accused stated that he was thirty-four and married with two children. MacPherson told the court that from 1923 to 1931 he had served in the Cameron Highlanders reaching the rank of staff sergeant. He was then an army reservist until 1938. When the war broke out MacPherson became a gun instructor for the RAF.

When questioned about firing on the police car the witness stated that he had no intention of killing anyone, only to stop the vehicle. MacPherson denied boasting of having brought down two Heinkels [German Bombers]. MacPherson again stated that he had orders from his wing commander to stop cars during air raids if he thought they were acting suspiciously. MacPherson denied that he was fuddled with drink, stating:

I am sorry that a man was shot and died. What I did was my duty and duty is not always a pleasure. I did not want to hurt anybody. There is no one more sorry than I am that an able man died.

When asked if he still thought what he did was right, he replied, '*Yes*'. With all the evidence heard, the Lord Justice Clerk addressed the jury:

It would not do for a soldier on leave to discharge a loaded rifle in the public street and take a human life and then seek to escape responsibility for his actions by saying that he thought he was doing his duty. . . It would be indeed a very serious thing if the community were to be at the peril of soldiers discharging their rifles when their challenges were unheeded.

It took the jury an hour to return with a verdict of guilty to a charge of assault and culpable *homicide* with a recommendation for mercy. The judge sentenced Alexander John McPherson to six-months' imprisonment.

It is worth noting that *The Scotsman*, which reported the trial and sentencing of MacPherson also reported on a trial at the High Court in Inverness. This shooting bore striking similarities to that involving Francis Lionel Harrington, a sentry in an army base in the North of

Scotland. Harrington shot and killed a passenger in a car that failed to stop near an army base. The military stated that:

Under present active service conditions a camp sentry charged with guarding a camp entrance was entitled between dusk and dawn to shoot to kill at any carload of passengers whose driver had not happened to hear three verbal challenges when passing along a public highway in quite suspicious circumstances.

The judge, Lord Keith, stated that it did not matter that the sentry was drunk at the time, as if drunk, he could do any more harm than he would be expected to do if he were sober. The court dismissed the case after deciding that the sentry tried at Inverness was only doing his duty.

Francis Lionel Harrington was on duty when he shot the passenger of the car and Alexander John MacPherson was not. Is a soldier in time of war ever off duty? It is easy to see why the RAF sergeant believed he was following orders on the night of 12 July in accordance with his military responsibility.

XXX
Sergeant William Gibson
Dumfries and Galloway Constabulary

22 May 1951

Robert Dobie Smith, shotgun in hand, loomed over his brother Andrew who sat at a table on the night of 22 May 1951. The armed man dictated while the sitting man wrote. On the paper, Andrew had printed, at his brother's request, the statement:

At the age of thirty, I have no further use of this world. Maybe I was born out of my century . . . When I go out of this door, I'll shoot the first policeman I see.

The brothers left the house and as they passed a phone box Robert ordered his brother to call the police to tell them that there was a mad man in Holme Avenue, Dumfries. As Robert walked away his brother pleaded with him to rethink his plan to shoot the first police officer he came across.

The police took the call and informed all officers on their beat to look out for an armed suspect. A passing police vehicle witnessed a man resembling the description given to them, acting suspiciously on the corner of Bank Street and the High Street. The three police officers travelling in the car got out and approached the suspect. Suddenly and without warning the man levelled a shotgun and shot Sergeant William Gibson in the face and head, mortally wounding him. Gibson died before he could receive any medical aid. Smith fired a second shot wounding Constable Andrew Hope in both arms. The third police officer, Robert Campbell, grappled with the shooter, talking later about disarming and arresting Smith and making the point when doing so that there are no Queensbury rules for such situations. Constable Campbell received the George Medal for his brave actions.

Constable Hope waved down a passing van delivering the early morning papers and asked the driver to take him to hospital. Hope passed out during the journey but recovered and walked into the hospital unaided. The driver, Alexander Nicol, later said:

Hope deserves a medal for what he did, both his arms were injured, he was losing a lot of blood and was in a state of collapse. But he stopped my van and insisted on helping the Sergeant into the police car.

On 24 July 1951, Robert Dobie Smith pled not guilty to charges of murdering Police Sergeant William Gibson and attempting to murder Constable Andrew Hope. The defence argued that Smith was insane and not responsible for his actions.

The accused's brother told the court of being forced to write the note at gunpoint. In the letter, Robert blamed his actions on the accidental death of a young family friend and a broken relationship. Asked why he did not try and disarm his brother, the witness replied that Robert was alert. The lawyer stated to Andrew Smith, '*You concluded that you were dealing with a madman with a loaded gun and any violent move by you might have created a very dangerous situation*'. Andrew replied, '*Yes*'.

Andrew also told the court that his brother had suffered attacks of blindness after injuring an eye at work. Smith noted this loss of sight worried Robert. A friend of the accused, James MacDonald of Irish Street, Dumfries, told the court that on 18 May (four days before the shooting) Robert had slipped in the street, struck his head on the pavement and briefly lost consciousness. Once home, Robert collapsed twice more that night. McDonald also stated that Robert had woken them in the early hours of 22 May. The accused had also made his wife write a note at gunpoint.

Sir David Kennedy Henderson, Physician Superintendent of the Royal Edinburgh Hospital for the Mentally Diseased, told the court that in his opinion, Robert Smith is in full possession of his senses, understands the charges against him and can converse and conduct himself in a sensible manner. The doctor also stated there is nothing to suggest Smith has been temporary of an unsound mind.

When cross-examined, the doctor admitted that he did not know Smith had collapsed or that the accused man had suffered three periods of unconsciousness within twenty-four hours. The doctor also admitted to being unaware that Smith's mother's family had a history of mental health issues and that Smith had attempted to commit suicide in the past. Dr Henderson acknowledged that if he had known the facts above it might have shown that the accused indeed did have mental problems.

Dr Arthur Gordon Hunter, Medical Officer of Dumfries Prison, thought Smith sane and fit to plead. Dr Peter McCowan backed Dr Hunter's testimony. McCowan stated that Smith was genuinely at a loss as to what he had done. The court discussed the amount and effect of the alcohol Smith had consumed that night and whether the accused man was drunk or mentally disturbed. This was the centre of debate addressed in court.

On 26 July, two doctors told the court that Smith was insane when he shot the police officers. Dr Angus McNiven, Superintendent of Gartnavel Mental Hospital, Edinburgh, said, that Smith was insane at the time of the offence. Dr John Caylor, a mental diseases consultant and lecturer in neurological medicine at Glasgow University, stated that he would have been prepared to certify Smith as insane.

Despite the contradictory evidence regarding Robert Smith's mental state, on Friday, 27 July, the jury found the prisoner guilty of murder. The judge, Lord Mackay, stated Smith had forced two people to write notes for him and even corrected a mistake in one of the letters. Lord Mackay also pointed out that a note that Smith wrote himself later appeared to be a goodbye note from a man who had a clear comprehension of what he was doing.

Lord Mackay sentenced Robert Smith to death. Smith, who had served in the Navy during the war, twice mentioned in despatches for bravery, became the first person to be executed in Edinburgh for twenty-five years. Smith's execution took place on 15 September 1951 in Saughton Prison, Edinburgh.

XXXI
Constable John McLeod
City of Glasgow Police

4 September 1952

Edwin Finlay doted on his infirm father, helping around the house he shared with his parents. Finlay carried his father down the three flights of stairs and out into the garden when the weather allowed. The eighteen-year-old liked to sit in the sheltered garden with his parents, enjoying the sunshine. One Monday morning, the pleasant and quiet youth made his way to the British Linen Bank branch on Argyle Street, Glasgow, where he worked as an apprentice clerk.

The next morning, Finlay failed to show for work. His family had no idea as to his whereabouts either. Finlay had fled to Dublin with £1,000 of the bank's money. The police investigating the case found out that Finlay liked to see seventeen-year-old Margaret Anne Frear on a Thursday evening. The couple were not in a relationship, but Finlay enjoyed watching fellow Sunday School teacher, Margaret, as she left the Western Lawn Tennis Club. The Glasgow Police sent two officers to the club on Thursday, 4 September 1952, hoping that Finlay would make an appearance.

Officers John McLeod and Thomas MacDonald thought this a routine job. The police believed Finlay to be out of the country. He had not been in trouble with the police before and any arrest made should be a straightforward affair. When the two police officers spotted the wanted youth, they could not have known that according to the *Daily Mail*, the young fugitive was armed like an Al Capone bodyguard. The wanted man had on his person, a .38 Webley Revolver, a .22 Spanish revolver and a .22 Beretta revolver, as well as a bandolier of ammunition around his left wrist and another around his body. In Finlay's pockets were three boxes of ammunition.

As the police officers approached, Finlay pulled out a pistol and shot Constable McLeod; then a shot hit and critically wounded Constable MacDonald. Another police officer arrived on the scene and Finlay ran off down Westbourne Road. The police who flooded to the area of the shooting soon cornered Finlay. The young man took out one of his guns and holding it to his head, shot himself. He died in the ambulance on the way to the hospital.

A nearby homeowner propped Constable McLeod against a wall but he did not regain consciousness. MacDonald, with a bullet lodged in his kidney, was still able to stand and talk. The dead officer left a wife and four-year-old son.

Shock spread through the city of Glasgow as news of the police officer's death circulated. The police issued a statement:

Finlay had never been in trouble with the police before and there was no reason to suspect when the officers were sent to locate him that he might be armed or dangerous [and they called the arrest] a routine job to pick up a suspect in a theft case.

The manager of the bank where Finlay worked called him a pleasant boy and stated he must have gone mad.

Finlay's old school friends and other youths in the area had a different opinion: they thought him wild and dangerous. His old school friends said that while at school Finlay carried a starter pistol to frighten his companions. If the police had been aware of the darker side to Finlay, a loving and doting son who was fascinated with guns, they might have been more cautious when approaching the wanted man.

PART TWO

Killer Cops

I

Police Constable Robert Sinclair

City of Glasgow Police

25 August 1865

At 7pm on the evening of Sunday, 27 August 1865, three young lads called into the Northern Police Office in Glasgow. The boys were James Wilson (an eighteen-year-old baker), George Hunter (aged sixteen) and Angus Campbell (a sixteen-year-old foundry moulder). They were anxious to report an incident that had taken place in the early hours of the morning of Friday, 25 August. The lads told their story to the duty sergeant. The officer realised that if what these young men had told them was true, then the allegation was so severe that someone more senior was going to have to deal with it.

Lieutenant Taylor was summoned to speak to the boys. They told him that they were all out of work and regularly did not have the money to pay for a bed for the night, so they often slept near the char kilns at Port Dundas. On the night in question, the three lads were sound asleep, along with their fifteen-year-old friend John Broadfoot, who was an out-of-work moulder. The boys were woken by police officers Robert Sinclair and Roderick McLachlan. The young lads all jumped up and fled. As they ran, the two police officers shouted at the fleeing boys to stop and gave chase. George Hunter then told the lieutenant that Constable Sinclair threw Broadfoot into the canal, shouting to the fleeing youngster, '*You beggar, I'll drown you*'.

Taylor realised that the seriousness of this statement called for Superintendent McFarlane. The boys were given a medical check-up and locked in the cells. The youngsters were willing and happy to be locked up for the night as it was warm, and they were given food to eat which of course would not have been the case if they were outside sleeping rough. At 8pm, Sinclair and McLachlan turned up to start their shifts. They were told of the allegation against them and both men were interviewed. The police officers denied any knowledge of the drowning, but they admitted having chased the boys by the canal. Given the gravity of the allegations, McFarlane thought it was best to hold the two police officers in the cells for the night. The next morning, the police and the boys went to the spot at Port Dundas where the young boy was said to have drowned. The canal was dragged and sure enough a body was found and identified as that of Broadfoot. The corpse was taken to the police station. Doctors Macleod and Renfrew were called to conduct a post-mortem. The doctors stated that they witnessed no signs of violence on the body and the cause of death had been drowning.

POLICE TRUNCHEONS

With the details of the story adding up, McFarlane went to speak to the two police officers again to see if they wanted to change their stories once faced with this new evidence. McLachlan stated that he and Sinclair did see if they could find any boys sleeping at the kilns in Port Dundas. The officer indicated that boys sleeping rough was a widespread problem in the area. On the night in question, they found the four boys sound asleep. The police officers drew their truncheons and used them to poke the boys in the chest to waken them. Once awake, the boys made a run for it and the two police officers gave chase. McLachlan stated that he was separated from Sinclair. He lost the two boys he was chasing and returned to see Sinclair standing and looking into the dark waters of the canal. McLachlan thought something was amiss with his companion and asked if a boy had fallen into the water. Sinclair replied that one had, and McLachlan said, '*Could you not save him?*'. Sinclair answered that he could not.

When McLachlan stated that they should report the matter, Sinclair argued that as no one had witnessed the boy falling into the canal, they must keep it quiet. But little did the two police officers know that the whole ghastly scene had been witnessed by James Wilson who had been hiding nearby. Wilson not only saw his friend John Broadfoot fall into the canal, but the boy also observed Sinclair use his baton to push the fleeing lad into the water after threatening to drown him.

With this information, the superintendent went to speak to Sinclair to see if he wanted to change his statement. Again, Sinclair denied seeing or being involved with the boy falling into the canal.

On Friday, 6 August 1865, Sinclair stood trial for the murder of John Broadfoot. James Wilson stated in court he had been sleeping at the kilns and was woken by a blow on the breast from a police baton. He told of running away from the constables chasing him and his friends and seeing Sinclair push Broadfoot in the middle of his back as he ran. This caused the young vagrant to fall into the canal. The witness said this was after the police officer had cried out that he would drown the fleeing boy. Another boy, George Hunter, supported Wilson's version of events.

The chief witness for the prosecution was Constable Roderick McLachlan. In the dock, he stated that he was a constable in the Glasgow Police Force and his beat took him near the canal basin. He reported that Sinclair was his partner, and they were in the habit of visiting the kilns about once a week in the summer. McLachlan stated that on the night of 25 August he and Sinclair spotted a group of boys sleeping on the west side of the kiln, about fifteen feet from the canal.

One police officer approached the boys from one side of the kiln and the other police officer from the other side in a pincer movement. McLachlan described how he woke Wilson by touching him with his baton and Sinclair did the same to Broadfoot. He added that the boys ran away, and he chased after Wilson, but he lost him. When he returned to find Sinclair, the police officer told him that a boy had fallen into the canal. McLachlan replied that they had better report the incident to which Sinclair responded, *'No, or else it would be death or life'*, implying that he may hang or be imprisoned for life if the matter were reported. McLachlan added that as Sinclair said this, he threateningly raised his baton. Again, the witness told of saying that they should report the boy falling into the water. Sinclair said, *'No'*. He argued that no one else had seen the boy fall into the water and that if they both kept quiet no one would ever know. McLachlan went on to say that Sinclair then said that if what had happened that night was discovered, they would both be in trouble.

Sinclair was found guilty of culpable homicide and sentenced to ten-years' penal servitude.

II
Police Constable James Kerr
Peeblesshire Constabulary

10 September 1892

Police Constable James Kerr of the Peeblesshire Constabulary was walking along the town's High Street in the early hours of Saturday, 10 September 1892. He saw a former colleague, ex-Police Constable John Scott, near the Town Hall. Scott had resigned from the Peebles force three weeks prior to move to Newcastle. Scott saw the police officer and started to swear and become aggressive towards Kerr. Ignoring the abuse, the constable told Scott to go home. Constable Kerr continued with his beat.

A brief time later, the police officer came across Scott near the parish church and again Scott became abusive. This time, Kerr threatened to arrest Scott. Suddenly, Scott attacked the police officer with a fire poker. As the blows rained down, Kerr shouted, '*Murder!*'. Kerr drew his baton and defended himself, hitting Scott across the head and felling him. Scott got up and ran off down the High Street. Kerr, shaking and shocked with what had just happened, also walked along the street as he had spotted Scott drop something as he ran. This was a fire poker, which Kerr recovered.

HIGH STREET, PEEBLES

Kerr made his way to the home of the force's inspector and reported the incident. Sergeant Bell and a constable went to the home of Scott to take him in for questioning, but he refused to go. The following morning the police again turned up at Scott's house, this time to arrest him; and his wife went to wake him. When she went into their bedroom, she found Scott lying dead in bed.

The dead man who was originally from Prestonpans had served in Peebles for two years. The twenty-six-year-old left a wife and child. The police detained thirty-six-year-old Kerr who had served in Peebles for eight years, pending the result of a post-mortem. When the results arrived, they showed that Scott died from a head injury caused by a blow from a police baton. The police arrested Kerr and a large crowd of shocked locals gathered outside the County Buildings, blocking the road.

Constable James Kerr's trial took place in Peebles on 14 October 1892. The Crown brought a charge of culpable homicide against Kerr. The first witness, Dr John Connell had assisted at the post-mortem. He said that a fractured skull and bleeding of the brain had killed John Scott. Connell also argued that such an injury might be caused by a baton if it were used with considerable force. When the defence asked if Scott had fallen while returning home and that the injury might have developed into a greater fracture, another witness, Dr McLean, asserted that there was nothing to suggest that the deceased had first received a minor fracture and then it had developed into a greater fracture.

James Miller told the court that just after midnight on 10 September he stood with another two men, Thomas Robertson and William Hunter, in the High Street at the head of School Brae. Kerr passed them and the police officer commented about it being a fine night. Soon afterwards, he saw Scott walking along the other side of the street. Scott crossed the street and said to the three men that Kerr was carrying a loaded stick.* Scott pulled out a poker and hollered that 'this was to defend himself'. Miller told the court that Scott seemed excited and expected conflict with Kerr that morning, saying to the three men that Kerr had accused him of pilfering on the railway.

The next witness, Mr Robertson, who was Keeper of the Conservative Club in Peebles, told of meeting Scott in the early morning of 10 September. Robertson said that when he asked Scott what was wrong with him, Scott replied that he was after that 'B— Kerr'. Scott showed the witness the poker he carried; he struck the pavement

---

* The police baton used by Kerr was thought by Scott to be weighed down at the top by something like lead, making it more effective.

with it saying that it would match Kerr's baton. Robertson then told the court that the conversation he had with Scott was of a hostile nature towards Kerr. When Kerr returned, the witness was afraid Scott was going to cross the street and assault the police officer.

William Hunter told of meeting Scott and asking him what the matter was. Again, Scott spoke of his hatred for Kerr. When Hunter said, '*You look well-armed*' to Scott, the ex-police officer showed the witness the poker. When Scott saw Kerr at the other side of the street, he shouted at him, '*I never was discharged from the Caledonian (railway) for pilfering and I never bought a fish from Mickie Moffat for a pint of whisky*'. Scott told Hunter that he hoped Kerr would go to the green as he would give him all the ways of it. Later that morning, Hunter told of Scott coming to his house and telling him, '*I must do that b— this nicht*'. Hunter had no doubts that Scott referred to Kerr.

The next to take the stand was Mrs Arrol, the wife of the Deputy Chief Constable. She said that on the morning of 10 September she heard someone using the ladle at the drinking well near the church followed by voices and the sound of a scuffle. She heard a cry, '*Help, murder!*' and when she looked out, she saw Kerr walking across the street.

Sergeant James Bell said that Kerr and Scott were on unfriendly terms when they served together in the police force. Bell told of hearing what he thought to be the cry of a heron out in the street. Then Kerr came into the station and told of being assaulted by Scott. Bell described Kerr as excited. The witness said Kerr looked like he had been in a great struggle. Bell thought that Kerr had stated that he could not get to his whistle, the excuse being that his cape was buttoned. Bell told the court that a buttoned cape would not prevent Kerr from accessing his whistle.

On cross-examination, Bell said that on the night of 9 September Scott came up to him and Constable Husband. Scott asked them if they knew of Kerr's whereabouts. Husband told him to go home and warned Scott that Kerr carried a loaded stick. Scott said to them that he would soon get something to defend himself. Constable Husband admitted in court that he told Scott about the loaded stick. Husband also stated that Scott had been out on other nights looking for Kerr.

Mrs Scott, the widow of the dead man, told that persecution by Kerr had driven her husband out of the police. The witness said on 9 September her husband told her as he sat by the fire that Kerr carried a loaded stick to murder him. She advised her husband not to get involved as no good could be got by fighting. Mrs Scott said that her husband then went out for a smoke and when he came back, mud covered his clothes, and he could not speak right. She said that he tried to tell her something but was not able.

The defence delivered a statement from Kerr stating that since Scott left the police force, he had been dreading an attack. Thomas Wright told the court that he had heard Scott swearing at Kerr and offering to fight. The witness said that Scott told him he intended to leave the Force, but he first intended to put Kerr out and to do for him before he left the town. When cross-examined, Wright admitted that he had attended the same school as Kerr in Musselburgh and was friendly with him.

The jury retired to consider all the evidence and they returned with a unanimous verdict of *'not guilty'*. Constable James Kerr had acted in self-defence, attacked by a man who harboured a grudge and who had told people in Peebles that he planned to use violence to get even with Kerr.

III
Police Sergeant John Jenkins
Stirlingshire Constabulary

18 April 1896

On the evening of Saturday, 18 April 1896, two plainclothes police officers walked along the High Street of Falkirk. The officers, Inspector Davidson and Sergeant Jenkins, were aware that as usual at 9pm on a Saturday the street was crowded. The police officers spotted a gang of boys near the 'Steeple', a landmark in the centre of

Falkirk. Remindful of the complaints from local shopkeepers about blocked access into the shops, the police officers approached the boys. When they got close, Sergeant Jenkins shouted at the boys, telling them to clear off.

The youngsters got a fright and scarpered in all directions. As one of the smallest of the boys ran past Jenkins, he took a swipe at the boy with the walking cane he carried. It hit the boy on the back of the legs as he scurried past. The officers were satisfied and continued with their beat.

THE STEEPLE, FALKIRK

The boy ran up the road and across the street and was heard, three times, to shout, '*Oh my leg!*' and, '*Oh ma!*' before collapsing. He was picked up by a passer-by and taken into a nearby shop. The boy, seven-year-old James Campbell, then expired.

On hearing the news about the young boy's collapse, the two police officers were shocked. Inspector Davidson and Sergeant Jenkins hurried to the shop. Meanwhile, rumours were flying about the town of Falkirk. Reports of a police officer killing a young lad spread through the streets. A large crowd soon assembled outside the shop where the body of young Campbell lay. The mob demanded Jenkins come out of the premises. Stones smashed the windows. The crowd threatened to storm the building, drag out the police officer and lynch him.

Things were getting out of hand as the crowd became increasingly threatening. Mr Gordon, Superintendent of Police, arrived with police reinforcements. Gordon satisfied the mob by promptly arresting Jenkins. A police guard with batons escorted Jenkins from the shop, dodging missiles of stones and having to fight back attempts by part of the crowd to get to the prisoner. The sergeant was taken to the police station and locked in a cell.

Police Sergeant John Jenkins stood before the judge in the Sheriff Court on Thursday, 14 May 1896 charged with culpable homicide. The police officer issued a plea of not guilty to the charges.

The first witness called was Dr Fraser, one of the doctors who conducted the post-mortem on young James. He told the court that the boy had suffered a heart attack. The medical man stated that from the state of the heart it was clear that any fright received by James would have stopped the heart. Dr Fraser commented that there were no external marks on the body and James had a half-healed ulcer at the back of his left hip. Fraser talked about the poor overall health of the deceased, calling James Campbell thin and emaciated. The doctor also stated that he had treated Campbell for influenza just before his death. During treatment, Dr Fraser found James to be a boy of a weak constitution, thin and sickly looking, nervous, and not well developed. Fraser also told the court that James's mother approached him and asked for a letter excusing her son from attending school. James suffered fainting fits, which was the reason for being absent from class.

On cross-examination, the doctor was asked if a blow on the legs of a healthy boy would result in death and Fraser stated that it would not. The prosecution asked if a blow to the old ulcer wound would be painful. The doctor replied that the area around the ulcer would have been extremely sensitive.

The next witness was the victim's mother, Mrs Campbell. When asked if James was frightened of police officers, she replied, 'He always went out of their way when he saw them'.

Inspector Davidson was the next to give evidence. He stated that on the night of 18 April he and the accused were walking towards the steeple. The officers saw a crowd of between eight to ten boys. The youngsters were all standing in the street looking at something; their heads were all down. As the two officers approached, Sergeant Jenkins shouted. Responding to the cry, all the boys scattered and, in their hurry to get away one of them tripped into the gutter. Two or three of the other youngsters fell over him.

When asked if he saw Sergeant Jenkins use his walking stick to hit any of the boys, the police officer stated that he did not see the accused use the stick on any boy. The witness did, however, admit that the police officer might have swung the stick without him seeing any blow. If the sergeant did strike a boy, it would only have been a tap said Davidson.

When questioned, Davidson admitted, if the accused had lifted his stick and struck the boy a blow, I would say he was exceeding his duty. Davidson revealed that he had in the past given boys a tap with a stick without thinking that he was exceeding his duty. Davidson also admitted that when he asked Jenkins if he had hit any of the boys, the sergeant answered that he had given a boy a bit of a tap.

Several boys were called to give evidence including the deceased's older brother John. All the boys reported seeing the police officer hit James Campbell with his walking stick, although the stories the youngsters told differed.

A statement from the accused police officer detailed the events that happened on the night of 18 April. Jenkins admitted tapping a boy on the hip as he rushed by. The police officer stated that the boy he struck was one of the biggest boys in the group, about twelve years of age. The police officer did not believe it was James Campbell, who was one of the smallest boys.

Superintendent Gordon told the court that before coming to Falkirk he had spent nine years in Aberdeen which was unlike Falkirk as all the police officers in Aberdeen carried sticks. When asked if he ever used a stick while serving in Aberdeen, the superintendent answered:

I frequently used a stick on juvenile offenders. [*Gordon then stated that he was*] requested by the parents of some boys to do this in preference to bringing them before the court. [*He also said*] of course, I took care to use the stick on a safe part of the body.

George Ballingall, a spirit merchant in Grangemouth and an ex-sergeant in the police, told the court that while serving in the Stirlingshire police, he applied the stick to youngsters. Ballingall also stated that the parents expected the use of the stick on their youngsters involved, explaining he was often blamed by parents for not using his stick more often.

The Crown decided to reduce the charge laid against Sergeant John Jenkins from that of culpable homicide to assault. The Crown now had to determine if an assault had been committed, whether a blow was given with any evil intent.

The defence counsel addressed the court stating that although he welcomed the lesser charge, he was quite convinced that the case would not have the same prominence if the accused had been a private person and not a police officer. The lawyer asked the court to consider the effect a prosecution for assault would have on the accused's career in the police. Again, the defence brought forward evidence from other police forces within Scotland to argue that carrying sticks to use on boys was customary practice. A statement from Mr Dewar, the Chief Constable and Burgh Prosecutor in Dundee, for example, detailed that when he served in Greenock, constables carried canes to *frighten the boys from pilfering sugar*. Dewar noted that, '*Not infrequently they gave the offenders a stroke with the stick while in the exercise of their duty'.*

During his summing up, the judge pointed out:

> *There might be violence necessary to drive a boy away from some criminal act in which he was engaged. However these boys were not engaged in what was a criminal offence. They were standing about doing what probably nine-tenths of the people about them were doing at the time; standing still.*

The judge stated that Jenkins was guilty of committing a technical assault as there was no intent to cause actual harm to the boy. He advised Sergeant Jenkins to use greater moderation in the future and stated that he would warn others to abstain from making use of like violence. Sergeant John Jenkins left the dock a free man.

IV
Police Constable James Ronald Robertson
City of Glasgow Police

27 July 1950

On the night of 27 July 1950, a woman's body was found on Prospecthill Road near the junction with Aitkenhead Road, Glasgow. She was dead. Initially, it looked like a simple hit-and-run accident. Little did the police know then that it was something much more sinister and would involve their own.

The woman was identified as forty-year-old Catherine McCluskey and she was rumoured to have been having an affair with Constable James Ronald Robertson. The police officer was picked up as part of a routine inquiry into the death. It was during this investigation the police found that the car Robertson was using was in fact stolen and showed signs of being involved in a recent accident.

Robertson was taken in for questioning and while he admitted driving a stolen car, he said that he had found it abandoned on his beat one night. The police officer stated he found fourteen car registration books in the car. He also claimed that he was not in a relationship with McCluskey but did give her a lift and was involved in a tragic accident which resulted in Catherine's death. Robertson claimed that on the night of 27 July 1950 he was on duty with his colleague. He told his partner that he had to nip off for two or three minutes. When the other police officer asked Robertson where he was going, he stated that he was going to see a blonde. He got into his car and drove away. He said that he happened to see McCluskey by chance. He stated that as he knew her, he stopped. She told him that she had been given a month's notice to get out of her house. McCluskey was going to see a friend in Neilston to arrange to stay there for a while. McCluskey asked Robertson if he could take her to her friend's house.

Robertson told how he refused to take McCluskey to Neilston as he was on duty but offered to drive her part of the way. She got into the car and he drove to Prospecthill Road. Once there, he changed his mind and decided that he must return to his beat. Robertson offered to take McCluskey back home first, but she refused, weeping, and then got out of the car. The officer started to drive off but then he stopped as he felt sorry for her. He decided to go back to see if she had changed her mind and would accept a lift home. Robertson reversed the car backwards at speed and said that he felt a jar. When he got out of the car, he could not see any sign of McCluskey. He stated that when he looked under the vehicle, he saw McCluskey's face below the car's running board. He admitted that he knew at once that she was dead, and he tried to pull her from under the vehicle. However, she was stuck fast. He then said that as he thought her clothing had become entangled in the drive shaft, he got into the car and reversed a little bit, then moved forward to free the trapped woman. She was left lying in the road at the back of the vehicle. Robertson stated that he panicked and drove off, leaving the body on the roadway.

James Ronald Robertson was arrested and tried for murder at the High Court in Glasgow in early November 1950. He denied being in

Catherine McCluskey's house in 1949 and being the police officer rumoured to be paying her a sum of money every week. The prisoner denied fathering a child with her. Asked to explain his reason for telling his colleague he was seeing a blonde when he left his beat on the night of the incident, the accused replied that it was a common light-hearted term used in the force, meaning that he was going away for a while.

Witnesses Mrs Elizabeth Coggans (the dead woman's sister), Mrs Grace Johnston and Mrs Rose O'Donnell seemed to refute Robertson's claim. Coggans told the court that her sister had two children and although she did not know who the father was, she had seen her sister speak to a police officer. Elizabeth Coggan picked Robertson out as that police officer in an identity parade. Johnstone said that Catherine told her that the father of one of her children was a police officer who paid her eight shillings a week. Rose O'Donnell talked of seeing Catherine in a car with a man in a police uniform and she also picked out the accused man in the dock as being that police officer.

On 11 November, Charles Alford Wicks, an automobile assessor, stated the damage to the Austin car involved in the incident showed no signs of having hit a pedestrian standing upright in the road. The vehicle did have damage and traces of blood and human hair to its underside which was consistent with the car reversing and running over someone or something lying in the road. Medical evidence brought forward by the Crown stated that it looked like Robertson had hit Catherine McCluskey over the head with his truncheon and driven over her more than once as she lay insensible on the road. A Dr Fiddes argued for the defence that the skull showed no evidence of being hit by a weapon.

On 13 November 1950, it took the jury of seven women and eight men just over an hour to find the accused guilty of murder. He was also convicted of stealing the car along with a radio and fourteen car registration books. The guilty man stood to attention in the dock and showed no sign of emotion as the judge, Lord Keith, sentenced him to death.

Robertson was hanged at 8.01am on 16 December 1950 in Barlinnie Prison, Glasgow. Ten people stood in the snow outside the prison gate to see the death notice being fixed to the prison gate at 8.15am. James Ronald Robertson was the first and only serving police officer to be executed by the state in Scotland.

PART THREE
Under Attack

I
Bombing of Loanhead Police Station
Midlothian

12 June 1881

The mining village of Loanhead stands south of Edinburgh. The village had been experiencing disturbances in the early summer of 1881. Unrest spread as workers employed in the pits clashed with the authorities over low wages and terms and conditions. Things had deteriorated to such a state that extra police officers were drafted into the area.

During the early hours of 12 June 1881, the police station was quiet. In the cells, languished several miners. Suddenly, a loud explosion shattered the station windows violently ending the stillness of the night. The duty officer ran out into the street where he found that along with the broken windows, a large part of the stone surrounding a cell window had been blown away.

In the middle of the road, lay an iron tube resembling a water pipe eight inches long and three in diameter; a couple of pounds in weight and sealed at one end. The tube had been filled with gun powder or other explosive material; perpetrators unknown had propped up the homemade explosive device against the window of one of the cells.

II
Under Attack, Roxburghshire

1886

Sometimes the police must think that they are unappreciated. The job of the police is to protect and serve the community. As we have seen at times, certain sections of society are openly hostile to the police. Imagine how police morale would suffer if it seemed nature itself turned on the Boys in Blue. That happened in Roxburghshire in 1886.

Alex Porter, the Chief Constable of Roxburghshire, inspected his men at Hawick. One officer looked decidedly dishevelled. When questioned about his appearance, the police officer answered that when on duty that morning near Branxholm, an owl had attacked him. The chief constable doubted this excuse, but the officer went on to describe an ongoing hostile attitude towards the police by our feathered friends. The police officer described an instance a month earlier when on his beat he heard a screech while passing a tree. Suddenly and out of nowhere, the police officer received a tremendous blow to the back of his neck. An owl had swooped down and ripped at the officer's skin with its claws and beak.

On a second occasion, the police officer walked towards the tree in a high state of alert. The officer kept his eyes forward and did not turn his back on the vicious beast's lair. An object flew from the sky and hit the officer on the face. The devil bird cut the constable on the face around his left cheek and under the eye. The police officer fought off his attacker and the owl flew over to the opposite side of the road and perched on a tree branch. Thinking it safe to beat a retreat, the officer turned to escape but again the owl swooped down, hitting the constable on the back. This time the owl flew off with a trophy of war in its claws, the police officer's cap. Another attack sent the police officer fleeing the scene of the crime.

The chief constable ordered an investigation and found other victims that had also suffered at the claws of this bird. Before the police could act, a gamekeeper solved the situation. He shot the owl, and the Roxburgh Police were able to close the case.

III
Circus Performers Attack a Police Station
Motherwell

18 June 1888

The wagons of Sanger's Circus arrived in Motherwell in the summer of 1888 bringing with it all the show's excitement and daring deeds. Each night, the inhabitants of Motherwell and the surrounding area packed into the big tent, to be amazed and entertained by a variety of performances.

The big top stood in a field in front of the town's Coursington Street. On the night of Monday, 18 June, Andrew Strang, a local foundry worker, fought with one of the men from the circus. Lee, the showman, drew a knife and stabbed Strang. When the police heard about the stabbing, police officers, Sergeant Shaw and Constable Harper made their way to Coursington Street to make an arrest. As the police arrested Lee, he sounded an alarm by creating a whistling sound like that of a parrot. Showmen appeared from all around the caravans and forcibly freed the prisoner. Lee was quickly recaptured, and the two police officers attempted to escort him to their station. During the fierce fighting, the circus men again sought to rescue Lee. A large crowd of around eighty or ninety circus entertainers hassled and harassed the police officers. The officers, with drawn batons, fought off attack after attack. In the *mêlée*, Constable Harper received a blow from a heavy weapon, breaking his arm between the wrist and elbow. Using his uninjured arm, Harper continued to fight his attackers before being knocked to the ground and having his arm broken again. Locals came to the assistance of the two police officers and a running battle took place until they reached the police station. The besieged officers sent an urgent plea for reinforcements from Hamilton, Wishaw, Hillhead, Stonehouse and Blantyre.

About a hundred men assembled outside the station and threatened to tear it down from the foundations if the police did not release the captive. Missiles rained down smashing windows in the building. Inside the station, the outnumbered police issued their civilian helpers with batons. The circus men started to rip down iron railings, turning them into weapons. Inspector Ross, the commanding officer, decided to take offensive action. When Ross gave a signal, the police and armed civilians charged from the station and assailed the showmen outside. The circus men, armed with pickaxe handles, iron bars, paling slabs and ten-foot poles topped with iron spikes, fought back. In the savage battle, Sergeant Shaw and another officer received severe wounds to the head. Shaw would lie in a severe condition for days after the attack. As the fighting continued, the police slowly forced the showmen back. Soon the circus men were running down Merry Street. Just then police officers from Hamilton turned up, shortly followed by reinforcements from Wishaw.

As the police flooded into Motherwell and regained control, a search for all those involved saw between thirty and forty arrests. Chief Constable McHardy commended the actions taken by the community and citizens of Motherwell in helping the police.

On 21 June, at Motherwell Police Court, eight men were found guilty of assault and breach of the peace and fined £5 with an alternative of thirty-days' imprisonment.

IV
Public Attack Glasgow Police Station

15 November 1901

On Saturday, 15 November 1901, police officers arrested a local nuisance – a man called Fraser – in Glasgow's East End. As the arresting party made their way to their police station, a large group of people followed pelting the police with stones and mud who then attacked the officers with sticks. The mob forced the police constables to take shelter in a baker's premises. As luck would have it, the shop had a telephone; a call brought police reinforcements. Before the extra police arrived, the crowd stormed the shop and wrecked it; other shops in the surrounding area were also damaged – the sound of breaking glass filled the street.

With the additional police at the scene, the officers took the prisoner to the station. The mob still launching missiles followed the arresting officers. They congregated outside the police station, shouting threats that they would smash into the building and free Fraser. The police responded by charging the crowd, which sent men, women and children fleeing in disarray.

The court convicted Fraser of causing a riot. He received a prison sentence of thirty days. Also fined were James McAllister and James Mains to the tune of twenty-one shillings (or thirty-days' imprisonment).

V
Clydebank Blitz
Glasgow

13-15 March 1941

The darkest period in the history of the Scottish Police Force took place between 13 and 15 March 1941. Britain and Nazi Germany were at war. Hitler's Luftwaffe was set upon destroying Britain's military infrastructure and industrial centres with a series of bombing raids. In the middle of March 1941, the Clydebank area became the target. The Luftwaffe sought the destruction of the Singer sewing machine factory then being used to manufacture armaments, John Brown's shipyard and the Beardmore engine works.

On the night of 13 March, the air raid siren wailed its banshee cry and searchlights scanned the sky over the town of Clydebank. The terrified population made their way to their nearest shelters as the drone of hundreds of bombers zeroed in on their targets. The first wave dropped incendiary bombs, causing fires that lit up the area. The following wave employed high explosive ordinance. The next night more German aircraft returned to attack the wounded town.

The bombs fell on industrial targets and civilian housing built around the factories and workplaces. In the devastation around 1,200 were killed and 1,000 injured. Out of 12,000 houses in the town, only eight remained undamaged after the raids; 48,000 people lost their homes.

The Clydebank Blitz and the air raid of 7 April 1941 took a toll on the local police force. The police officers lost during the Clydebank Blitz are named below:

13 March 1941

Constable William Steven Dickson, City of Glasgow Police
Constable Thomas Marlin, War Department Constabulary
Sergeant Peter Hunter Johnstone, War Department Constabulary
Sergeant William Robert Lyons, War Department Constabulary
Special Constable Donald MacDonald, City of Glasgow
Police Constable Percival John (Jack) Deegans, Air Ministry
Constabulary

14 March 1941

Special Constable John Gerard MacKrell, City of Glasgow Police
Special Constable James Williamson, City of Glasgow Police
Special Constable Thomas Hamilton, City of Glasgow Police

7 April 1941

Constable William Dalgetty, Paisley Burgh Police

These officers died while involved in individual acts of bravery, lost amid the death and destruction of war. The Scottish Police Memorial, Tulliallan (Police Scotland College) simply states these men *'died as a result of enemy action during an air raid'*.

THE SCOTTISH POLICE MEMORIAL, TULLIALLAN

PART FOUR

Lucky Escapes

I
Police Constables James Chalmers and Donald Fraser
Leith Burgh Police

6 November 1878

Police Constable James Chalmers walked along Bridge Street, Leith. As he passed a china shop, the police officer heard a report of gunfire, following which he felt a searing pain in his leg and then collapsed. A shot from inside the premises had hit the police officer in the leg.

Inside the building, Patrick Ferguson and his sister, the owner of the shop, had been arguing violently. When Ferguson noticed the police officer outside in the street, he fired at the officer.

Police officers made their way to the shop where two men informed the constables that they had disarmed Ferguson and he had fled the shop to a nearby yard. The police surrounded the yard and cornered the wanted man in a loft. Ferguson, armed with a knife and hatchet, shouted threats down to the officers. The armed man kept the police at bay for over an hour until Detective Alex Main and Ferguson's brother managed to gain unseen access to the loft. The armed man, realising that the police had managed to get behind him, charged down the staircase towards the police. Detective Angus McKay was on his way up the stairs and on coming down, Ferguson knocked down the police officer, who landed heavily. Constable Donald Fraser tried to stop Ferguson, but the deranged man stabbed the police officer three times in the shoulder during the struggle. Main received a knife wound to the hand.

The police managed to overpower Ferguson and after manacling him they put him in a wheelbarrow and wheeled him to Charlotte Street Police Station.

Patrick Ferguson stood in the Leith Police Court in a wild and excited state, muttering angrily during the reading of the charges. The authorities decided to take the case to the High Court. At his trial in Edinburgh on 24 February 1879, the court agreed that clearly the prisoner had a mental illness and sentenced Ferguson to strict custody at Her Majesty's pleasure.

II
Police Constable William Barron
Morayshire Constabulary

26 May 1905

On 26 May 1905, the police received a call of a disturbance at the house of James Stewart Craigie at 57 High Street in Rothes, near Elgin. Two police officers, Constable William Barron and Constable Robertson, made their way to the address. When the officers arrived at the house, Mrs Craigie informed the officers that her husband was a little quieter and she said that she did not want to press any charges against him. The police officers started to walk down the street when Mrs Christie shouted after them, '*He has got a gun!*'.

LEE-ENFIELD RIFLE

The officers returned to the house where Constable Barron entered the building and tried to reason with the armed man. Craigie aimed a Lee-Enfield rifle and deliberately fired it at the police officer. The bullet hit Barron in the shoulder and passed through the body before exiting through the police officer between his third and fourth rib. The projectile then hit and passed and through an interior wall and grazed the slippers of the next-door neighbour sitting at his fireside.

The police arrested Craigie, a military volunteer, who had been out of work for a time. It may have been a coincidence that Craigie had worked as a licensed grocer but had had his licence revoked. One reason for the removal of his licence was that he sent officer Barron a bottle of whisky at Christmas a year or two before the shooting. At his trial at the High Court in Inverness, Craigie pled guilty. He received a sentence of three-years' penal servitude.

III
Lance Corporal G F Jackson
Military Police

17 April 1919

On the night of 17 April 1919, Lance Corporal G F Jackson, a military police officer, was walking along North Frederick Street, Glasgow, when he stopped to speak to a sailor. The two men had words and the police officer turned to walk away. As the police officer walked off, the sailor took out a revolver and shot Jackson in the back of his shoulder. Later, a body resembling the shooter and identified as Gilbert Sinclair was found on the bank of the Forth and Clyde Canal. He had shot himself in the head.

IV
Police Constable Alexander McKay
Lanarkshire Constabulary

28 October 1920

At 1.30am on the foggy night of 28 October 1920, a chauffeur-driven car stopped, and the driver informed two police officers about a group of men acting suspiciously. Constable Alexander McKay and Constable Gray went to investigate. The police officers saw two men walking towards them on Langside Road, Bothwell. The officers stopped the men and asked one for his name. The man replied Rodgers. Constable Gray, with his flashlight in hand, grabbed the man by the arm and asked him what he had in his pocket. At this, the man wrestled free and ran away. Gray told his colleague that Rodgers had a revolver on his person.

Just then several men appeared and stood right across the road in front of the constables. One of the men told the officers to put their hands up, exclaiming *'You are going to be done tonight!'*. The man who spoke pulled out a bayonet and the police officers drew their batons.

A man barked out a military-style order, *'Draw revolvers, fire!'*. The men drew out their guns and without any hesitation fired at the police officers. Constable McKay was hit twice in the arm and once in the body. The stricken officer fell onto the road and another 'small man' stood over him and fired two shots at close range at the prone police officer. Both shots missed. Another man stepped forward and gave the injured police officer a savage kick. The unhurt Gray fled to get assistance.

BOTHWELL BRIDGE

When Gray sounded the alarm, the police responded quickly but could find no trace of the men. The thick fog that cloaked the countryside did not help the police attempts to find the culprits. The next day, a schoolchild found a magazine for a government issue .455 revolver. The police found a bullet under a tree near Bothwell Bridge on 6 November.

From the start of the investigation into this shooting the police linked it with Sinn Fein. In a report on the incident on 29 October 1920, the *Dundee Evening Telegraph* called the area around Uddingston,

Bothwell, Blantyre and the surrounding villages a hotbed of Sinn Fein activity. The police spent their time interviewing men in the area who were known to be sympathetic to the Irish Republican cause.

Another view detailed in the *Dundee Evening Telegraph* was that the police had been deliberately targeted. The paper said that on the previous day the local police force had arrested eight miners for stealing coal from the local pit. There was a miners' strike going on at the time and tensions between the striking miners and the authorities would have been high. Although the paper printed this story, it also stated this theory to be no more than local gossip.

Several men were arrested and stood trial at the High Court in Glasgow on 7 February 1921. The men in the dock were Charles McGinn, Robert McErlane, James Rodgers, Patrick Clark, Patrick Martin, Patrick Moan and William Docherty. Martin and Moan pled not guilty while the other five men stated that they had an alibi for the time of the shooting. Witnesses returning from the local Masonic Lodge told of seeing a group of men and a lorry at the scene of the attack on 28 October. Not one witness could identify the prisoners as being the men out on the night in question.

A water inspector stated that he met Clark and Rodgers going uphill towards Bothwell that night. He admitted that as the miners were on strike it was not unusual to see striking workers out late at night. An Inspector Kemp who arrested Clark stated that Clark denied being in Bothwell on 28 October. The police officer who arrested Rodgers said he found the wanted man at home in the early morning of the gun attack. The police officer told the court that the prisoner's boots were wet and had grass sticking to the upper parts. The police officer said to Rodgers, '*You must have been out?*' to which Rodgers replied, '*Aye Sergeant!*'. In the police station Martin admitted to being at the scene of the shooting but stated that he bolted when the firing started and had nothing to do with it. Martin confessed to being a member of Sinn Fein.

On the second day of the trial, Detective Sergeant Much from Cambuslang said the lorry seen in Bothwell on the night of the shooting had been traced to a garage in Petershill Road, Glasgow. McErlane was arrested in connection but denied that he or the vehicle had been in Bothwell on 28 October. McErlane stated that the Fiat lorry was in the garage being repaired on 27 October. The police admitted that the vehicle was in a dismantled state when they went into the garage but when the police checked the lorry, they could not find anything mechanically wrong with it.

The next prisoner to take the stand was Charles McGinn, the alleged leader of the gang. He stated that he had been in Dublin on the night in question and he had read about the shootings in Bothwell in an Irish newspaper. Witnesses were brought over from Ireland to verify McGinn's alibi.

In court, Clark denied being involved in any shooting and he stated that he was a fifty-year-old miner and a widower with six children. Clark admitted being out with Rodgers on the evening of the 27 October but stated he was in bed later that night. He claimed that he had never had a revolver in his hands or even seen one until shown a gun in court.

On the third day, the daughter of Patrick Clark took the stand. She told the court that on the night in question her father had come home at 9.30pm and went to bed at 11pm. She detailed that, as she slept in the kitchen and her father would have had to exit the house by walking through the kitchen, she was positive her father could not have gotten out without awakening her. She stated that the kitchen door made a noise when it opened.

Patrick Martin told an unusual story when he addressed the court. He stated that on the night of the shooting he was at a dance with his wife at Craigneuk. While at the dance someone approached him and asked if Martin could take him and some other men to the Palace Colliery, Hamilton. He told them that as he had worked there, he knew the way and would take them. Martin took seven or eight men, one of them wearing a police uniform, to a farm. Martin told the court that he started to think something was amiss and he asked to be allowed to go home. One man drew out a revolver and threatened him.

The party arrived at a large building with a crowd of men standing around. Martin explained that he heard a shout that someone was coming, and seeing his chance, he nipped through a hedge and started to run. He heard someone behind him threatening to shoot and then the sound of shots fired. Martin said he made his way to the home of a man called Bryson and the police arrested him there.

Martin admitted that he had once been a member of Sinn Fein but had left the organisation. When asked why he was no longer involved, Martin told the Court that he worked every day until 3pm and he did not take a great interest in them and had only been at three or four meetings. Asked by Lord Anderson, *'Do you say that when a perfect stranger came to you, while you were enjoying yourself at a dance and asked you to walk three miles with him to show him a place, you did it?'*, Martin replied, *'Yes, I have done as much before'*.

The court revealed that the reason Sinn Fein members had been out on that night was to break into the Bothwell Drill Hall which contained a cache of rifles. The hall, however, contained fewer weapons than the Irish Republicans thought.

The jury retired and returned after twenty minutes. Charles McGinn, James Rodgers, Patrick Martin and Patrick Moan were found guilty. Robert McErlane, Patrick Clark and William Docherty received verdicts of not proven. McGinn, who despite only being nineteen was regarded as being the leader, received ten-years' penal servitude. The rest received eight years.

In his book, *The IRA in Britain 1919–1923, In the Heart of Enemy Lines* (2014), Gerard Noonan argued that after this shooting the Chief Constable of Lanarkshire requested that his officers be armed to protect themselves. The Secretary of State for Scotland approved this and armed the Lanarkshire police for six months.

V
Police Constable William Petrie
Edinburgh City Police*

16 January 1923

In January 1923, the police were keeping a close eye on a garage in Jamaica Street Lane, Edinburgh, for inside that premises lay a stolen two-seater Calcott (an automobile made in England). The vehicle had been stolen weeks before when parked outside the British Station Hotel in the city. A police officer passing on his beat had spotted the car through an open garage door. Since then the police had kept a constant watch on the building, working in shifts and hoping to catch the car thieves.

On the night of 16 January 1923, the police spotted two men approach the garage. When one man opened the door and entered the building the police outside knew they had their men. Two officers, Detective Constable Joseph Marshall and Constable William Petrie, walked across the road toward the garage. As the officers moved in to make an arrest, one man drew a revolver and fired at the police officers, wounding William Petrie in the shoulder. The gunman fled the scene. The police arrested the second man, Alexander Joseph Davidson, at the scene of the shooting.

The police found out the gunman's name, identifying him as twenty-five-year-old Glaswegian Charles Watson. The man who was arrested in Jamaica Street Lane took the police to the wanted man's lodgings in Barony Street, Edinburgh. Watson had barricaded himself in his room and knowing the wanted man to be armed and dangerous, the police prepared for a long siege. With no response from the man in the building, the police entered and found Watson dead – he had shot

---

* I could not find any account detailing in which police service William Petrie served. I have noted where the crime took place and have taken an educated guess that William served in the Edinburgh City Police which served the city from 1805–1975. I have done the same for the case Police Sergeant George Shannon. www.britishpolicehistory.uk.

himself. A letter addressed to his sister lay by his side.

It is worth telling a little bit of Charles Watson's background, for the theft of the car and shooting at the police did not come from a life of poverty and deprivation. Watson's father owned a successful restaurant and a billiard hall in London Street and Argyle Street, Glasgow, respectively. Upon his father's death, Watson inherited a sizeable fortune.

This wealth seems not to have kept Watson from a life of crime. He was born Alfred Charles Watson in Largs in 1899 and he lived in the seaside town for his first eighteen years. As an adult, he drifted into a life of crime, serving six months hard labour for stealing a car in Pollokshields. He also received a £2 fine for walking into a book-maker with a revolver and demanding £5. When asked what he would do if the police came after him again, he answered, '*The police will never again take me alive*'.

When Watson's sister came from Glasgow to Edinburgh to identify her brother's body, the police gave her the letter her brother had addressed to her. The letter provides an insight into the mind of Charles Watson just before he killed himself:

My dear Sister

God forgive me for this, but, my very dear sister, it has been forced on me by circumstances. I am absolutely broke, and as I could not get work, something had to be done. You will understand the position. I tried hard since I came back, but found it impossible. If I could only have some assistance, everything would have been A1, but every one of my friends seems to want to get something, not to give. Of course, this is the way of the world, when you are down to keep you down. What has happened to-night, Mary dear, I can remember only in a hazy sort of way. Now, Mary, I intend to shoot myself. It is the best thing for me to do. At times I really think I am mad, and I don't doubt it now. I seem to get relief in contemplating this. The worry this while back has got on my nerves, and you know I cannot stand it. I wish to God I had been killed in the war. It would have saved you all this sorrow, Mary.

Go and see your aunt, Mary, and see if she can do anything for you. I think she will in the circumstances. I have no money left, dear, but have two silver cups, also the belt of Scotland lying at – (an address) – and also some effects. They are yours.

I am heartbroken at all this trouble I have caused you, dear little sister, and hope somebody with a heart will give you a hand and not do as they have done to me.

Well, dear Mary, my time on this earth is limited now, and I must hurry. God forgive me, and also you Mary. I think I must be mad to do this, but I am distracted. Well, Mary, good-bye, and also think kindly of your broken hearted brother.

With all my love, your distracted brother, Alf.

Watson left another letter addressed to the Procurator Fiscal, in which he stated he did not mean to shoot the police officer but merely fired to frighten him. In this letter, Watson is convinced he has shot Constable Petrie dead and believed he would hang if caught.

The other man arrested at the garage, Alexander Joseph Davidson, denied knowing the car was stolen. Davidson received a twelve-month prison sentence.

VII
Police Constable William McLeod
City of Glasgow Police

1 January 1932

In the early hours of New Year's morning 1932, off-duty Police Constable William McLeod had been enjoying the festivities at home at 230 Anniesland, Glasgow. At around 4.30am, McLeod decided to get a bit of fresh air and go for a walk. He did not intend to go far as he still had on his slippers when he left the house. As her husband had not returned by 6.30am, Mrs McLeod went out to look for him. She found her husband lying in the street semi-conscious, with blood from a gunshot wound in his leg turning the black tarmac red. After she shouted for help, two men ran to assist Mrs McLeod.

William McLeod subsequently told of coming across two men fighting in the street. When he tried to appease them one of the men drew out a revolver and shot him.

The *Scotsman* from 2 January 1932 gave a different account of the shooting under the heading *'Glasgow Policeman Wounded'*. The *Scotsman* stated that McLeod received a gunshot accidentally. It said that as McLeod and two companions had a look at the revolver, it went off. That account does not tie in with the stories printed in the *Aberdeen Press and Journal*, *The Dundee Courier* dated 2 January and the *Dundee Evening Telegraph* on the day of the shooting, which all reported Mrs McLeod finding her husband lying on the street. If the officer received the wound by accident as he looked at the gun with two companions, why would they leave him lying in the gutter where he might well have bled to death? Surely if it had been a simple accident, they would have sought medical assistance.

VIII
Police Sergeant George Shannon
Edinburgh City Police

3 April 1942

Police Sergeant George Shannon walked his beat in the early hours of the morning on 3 April 1942. Edinburgh in wartime would have been blacked out. There would be no streetlights to offer a protective glow around the police officer as he walked along George Street, one of the city's premier shopping areas. Suddenly the unmistakable sound of smashing glass violated the peace of the morning. Shannon walked in the direction of the noise with his torch in his hand, while trying to shield the light. He was fearful that any German bombers flying in the vicinity of Edinburgh could spot an escape of light to use as a guide to the whereabouts of the city.

The police officer found a smashed window of a shop in nearby

Hanover Street. The shop belonged to the Anglo-Canadian (Edinburgh) Fur Company. A dark figure could be seen inside the window crouching down amongst the expensive fur coats. The officer ordered the man to come from the shop. Shannon took hold of the thief who seemed to have accepted the situation, saying to the police officer, '*It's a fair cop*'. Shannon put his whistle to his lips to call for assistance, but the man broke free, took out a gun and shot at the police officer. A bullet entered Shannon's right leg just above the ankle. The man fired another shot at the police officer which missed, before grabbing half a dozen fur coats and running off into the darkness.

Two patrolling police officers ran in the direction of the whistle and gunshots. A pile of fur coats lay abandoned, strewn over the pavement. The fallen police officer gave a description of the man who shot him before being taken to hospital. The police officer described the wanted man as about twenty, about 5' 9" tall, round faced and dressed in a grey sports jacket with flannel trousers. He was also hatless. Witnesses reported seeing a powerful Vauxhall car speed through the city soon after the shooting.

The police arrested twenty-one-year-old ship's steward Christopher Anderson McKinley at his Edinburgh address in connection with the shooting. On Monday, 20 July 1942, the Lord Justice-Clerk, Lord Cooper, sentenced the accused to seven-years' penal servitude for shooting the police officer. He also received an additional three months for having an automatic pistol and twenty-four rounds of ammunition without having a firearms certificate. Christopher McKinley also admitted further charges of breaking into a dozen houses in Edinburgh, Glasgow and Bathgate.

PART FIVE

In the Line of Duty

I

Police Sergeant James Watson

Dundee City Police

18 September 1870

Just before midnight on 17 September 1870, the streets of Dundee were quiet. Those out noticed the smell of smoke, which had been carried on the breeze. A brief time later, thick smoke hung low over Dock Street. Several people went to investigate and found it was emanating from a warehouse in Trades Lane belonging to Messrs John Gordon & Co, spinners and manufacturers. The warehouse was packed full of flax, tow and jute, with smoke billowing from its roof. Suddenly flames shot into the air from three points at the top of the building.

DUNDEE DOCKS

The brick walls in the warehouse reached eighteen feet in height from floor to roof. Other warehouses filled with equally flammable material surrounded the building on fire. Separated by a gable wall from the burning building was a large store owned by the Dundee Public Warehouse Company. At the back of the building was a twelve-foot-wide narrow lane, the only thing separating the source of the fire from a vast storage of combustible material. This fire could potentially devastate a considerable portion of this great industrial city from Trades Lane to Commercial Street and down to the docks.

Soon the city fire brigade arrived at the scene and news of the blaze spread through Dundee. Crowds left their homes and made their way to investigate or offer help. Dundee Police Force soon sprang into action. Superintendent MacKay arrived at the scene and soldiers from the barracks arrived to lend a hand. MacKay immediately ordered his men to keep the crowds back and at a safe distance. The firefighters pumped water from the Seagate but the heat from the flames turned the water from the hoses into steam before it could have any effect. The *Dundee Courier* of Monday, 19 September, gave a good eyewitness feel of the events that night:

The scene at this time was one of terrible grandeur. The roof of the building fell in with a crash, amid a shower of sparks and burning fragments. After a moment the flames again shot up with renewed fury, while the hissing of the water and the heavy flap of the great sheets of flame were the only sounds that broke upon the dull murmuring of the crowd.

With most firefighters engaged at the front of the building, Fire Captain Fyffe ordered men to take a hose along the narrow lane at the back. A team of firefighters worked at setting up a hose in the alley while others found and propped a wooden ladder up against the wall of the blazing building. Members of the public ran up the lane, rescued two carts and took them down to Dock Street out of immediate danger.

A large crowd packed into the lane to watch the proceedings. Realising the danger to this group of onlookers bunched into the narrow road, the police chief sent an Inspector Renny and Sergeant Watson round to clear the public from the area. In the lane, two firefighters connected the ladder to prop up against the wall. Suddenly and without warning, a large section of brick wall came crashing down, burying all underneath. News of this disaster reached those at the front of the building. People flocked to the rear to help in the rescue of those trapped under the debris.

The intense heat made any rescue attempt extremely difficult and to add to the hazards, the bricks lying on top of the trapped people glowed red hot. Two firefighters who narrowly escaped the collapsing wall themselves tried to pull the fire hose from underneath the masonry. Unable to get the hose free, they cut it and sprayed the hot bricks. For three hours men and boys laboured to free those trapped. They took the dead and injured to a makeshift hospital established in East Dock Street Station.

In the station, the railwaymen removed cushions from the train carriages to make the wounded more comfortable. Doctors from all over the city arrived at the scene to treat those in need of attention. The medical men sent the casualties either home or up to the infirmary in horse-drawn cabs. The doctors treated those who had burned their hands while trying to remove the pile of bricks.

Back at the scene, a cry of '*Where is Fyffe?*' broke out amongst the firefighters. Their chief seemed to be missing. Captain Fyffe's son, also a firefighter, began looking for his father and someone told him that the fire captain might be in the hospital. Fyffe's son went to the infirmary but could not find his father. He tried going home to see if his father had made his way there, again without luck.

Captain Fyffe's helmet was later discovered among the rubble, followed by his dead body. Tears rolled down the dirty cheeks of firefighters as they carried their captain's corpse to the fire station.

Moments before the rescuers discovered the body of the firefighter, they found the remains of Police Sergeant James Watson. He and Inspector Renny had been trying to clear the lane of spectators when the wall collapsed. Inspector Renny and two other firefighters were among the injured. Just before the body arrived at her house, the superintendent made his way to Watson's home to convey the terrible news to the officer's wife.

Robert Jenkins, a twenty-year-old labourer and twenty-eight-year-old Bernard Clark also lost their lives that night, both severely burned. Twenty people were injured, the youngest being fourteen-year-old Henry Fay who had his hands burned while clearing rubble.

As late as Tuesday, 20 September, three days after the fire, when workers lifted debris, the wind would suddenly ignite sections of the smouldering building. Firefighters stood ready to extinguish these small fires when they broke out.

The day after the fire, Sergeant Watson's funeral took place and the whole City Police Force assembled in uniform at the police station. Along with the police were about twenty of the city's lamplighters. Large crowds took to the street and hung out of tenement windows as the body of the police veteran travelled from his home in Albion Passage, Overgate, to the Western Cemetery. Twenty-one cabs containing the mourners followed the hearse to the graveyard.

The city paid Sergeant James Watson's widow £20 annually, to *'put her beyond poverty during the rest of her life'.*

II

Police Inspector James Christie
Edinburgh City Police

21 March 1896

On the evening of Saturday, 21 March 1896, just after the change of shift at the West Port Police Station in Edinburgh, Inspector James Christie, walked out the station to head for home. His journey took him through the city's Grassmarket where Christie's attention was caught by a group of men noisily emerging from a pub.

Christie made his way over and tried to move this disorderly group. Suddenly the police officer cried out, clutched his chest, and collapsed. The fifty-nine-year-old inspector, a native of Gartly, Aberdeenshire, with over thirty-four-years' service in the Edinburgh police force, had a heart attack and died almost immediately.

When the papers reported on the news of the inspector's death, they give good indication of the police practices of the day. The *Edinburgh Evening News* was a good example:

Though somewhat hasty in temper he was generous and warm-hearted and gave many a fourpence to pay for a bed or sixpence for a

THE GRASSMARKET, EDINBURGH

supper to those who were 'down on their luck'. The mischievous urchins in Central Edinburgh had a healthy respect for Christie's stick. If their wickedness was not too great, he preferred to execute judgment on them then and there with his cane rather than 'run them in' and have them fined, knowing that their parents would have to pay. When a serious row was on late on a Saturday night, Christie's presence with his stick was always as good as three men.

Christie's use of the stick is worth remembering when thinking about Sergeant Jenkins in Falkirk, a month after Christie's death.

The same paper also stated that James Christie received a medal from the Royal Humane Society for rescuing a dog which had fallen through ice on a frozen loch.

III

Police Sergeant George Gibson
Hamilton Burgh Police

17 July 1903

Police Sergeant George Gibson of the Hamilton Burgh Police Force arrived with another constable at Hamilton North railway station on Saturday 18 July 1903. The police had come to sort out a disturbance on one of the platforms. The sergeant managed to quieten down those involved and persuaded one man to board a train. Things now quiet, the sergeant turned around and collapsed into the arms of the constable. Gibson died in a waiting room at the station soon afterwards. He had suffered a heart attack.

IV

Police Constable William Balfour Urquhart
Aberdeen City Police

22 March 1904

The shopkeepers were sick and tired of the behaviour of gangs of young boys in the Holburn area of Aberdeen. These youths congregated around the front of the shops near the junction of Great Western Road and Holburn Street. The boys aged between ten and fifteen entertained themselves by removing the billboards outside the shops and swapping them. They would push and shove each other in the shop doorways and shout at each other and customers as they entered or left the premises. The youngsters also targeted the gardens in the area, taking part in what the *Aberdeen Press and Journal* of Thursday, 24 March 1904, called malicious mischief.

The shop proprietors called and complained to the police often. The police sent regular patrols to the area, but the increased police presence did not have any effect. The youths would goad the officers and enjoyed getting a chase from the bobbies.

Constable William Balfour Urquhart, a forty-nine-year-old police officer, served in the Aberdeen City police force. He knew the boys causing the trouble and the *Aberdeen Press and Journal* reported that Constable Urquhart acted kindly towards them and that they took advantage of the officer's leniency. On 22 March, the youths coaxed Constable Urquhart into chasing them. While doing this, the officer collapsed and died.

V
Police Inspector John Scott
East Lothian Constabulary

27 August 1906

Police Inspector John Scott was instructed to check the railway line near Dunbar following an attempt to wreck the London East Coast Express train. This effort to derail the train involved laying heavy pieces of metal on the line. Since that failed attempt two months previously, the inspector and a detachment of his men would patrol the railway line nightly. On the night of 28 August 1906, a passing train hit Inspector John Scott, killing him instantly.

VI
Police Superintendent Charles McIntyre
Argyllshire Constabulary

2 June 1908

Superintendent Charles McIntyre of the Argyllshire Constabulary escorted a prisoner from Oban to Duke Street Prison in Glasgow. After arriving in Glasgow, the pair took a cab to the prison. During the journey, the 68-year-old police officer took ill and died. The prisoner stayed with the police officer and did not make any attempt to escape.

VII
Police Sergeant Samuel MacLean
Dunbartonshire Constabulary

27 August 1926

A young woman named Isabella Wright looked up and smiled when she saw the customer enter the tobacconist and sub-post office in Kilbowie Road, Clydebank on Thursday 26 August 1926. The man walked to the counter and asked for a notebook. Suddenly he raised an arm and brought a lemonade bottle wrapped in a racing newspaper crashing down on the woman's head. Stunned and on the verge of collapse, Isabella managed to scream.

KILBOWIE ROAD, CLYDEBANK

In another part of the town, Elizabeth Winifred Curran stood by her window at 31 Hamiltonhill Road. She and her boyfriend planned to go out and buy cakes for their wedding breakfast which was due to take place the coming Saturday. The woman paced up and down by the window, fretting. Her sweetheart, James Jackson, should have arrived at her house at 2.30pm that afternoon. Jackson had gone to arrange the taxis for the wedding party and draw his wages from the post office. Perhaps Miss Curran worried that her fiancé had second thoughts about the upcoming wedding as he had joked the night before that he had only two days of freedom left.

The man in the post office fled the scene and the screams of the injured woman caught the attention of passers-by in the crowded street. Realising something to be wrong, a group who had witnessed a man run out of the post office gave chase.

Mrs MacLean looked out of her window at 26 Livingstone Street and saw a disturbance down the road. She thought that something must have happened at the railway carriages used at the time for housing. Then she saw her husband, Sergeant Samuel MacLean. He entered the house, smiled, threw down his cape and dashed out again without saying a word.

MacLean flagged down a passing van and as he jumped into the passenger's side, he ordered the driver to drive along the Glasgow Road. MacLean hoped to intercept the fleeing man. The van driver, police sergeant and ten other men in the back of the vehicle sped along the road when a tyre blew with a loud bang. The driver, unable to control the vehicle, crashed into an oncoming tram. Crushed between the van and tram, MacLean received a broken leg and a fractured thigh. Eight civilians were also injured. MacLean was taken to the Western Infirmary where he died from his injuries the next morning.

Frantic with worry and convinced something terrible must have happened to her boyfriend, when Elizabeth Curran was told of the accident, she became convinced that James must have gotten caught up in it. She made her way to the hospital looking for him, certain that if he was involved in the crash, she would find him there. Disappointed and at a total loss as to his whereabouts after having no luck in the Western Infirmary, Curran went home. Shortly after arriving at her house, two detectives arrived and told Elizabeth that they had arrested her husband-to-be in connection with a robbery at the post office. The crowd had chased the suspected robber and caught up with him by the canal. Curran hurried to the police station to hear details of the arrest. Later, when she was allowed to see Jackson, he said to her, *'Don't worry Lizzie, everything will come all right. I wasn't even in the shop'.*

James Jackson pled guilty at the High Court in Glasgow on 18 October 1926. He received a sentence of five-years' penal servitude.

VIII
Police Constable Sydney Hussey Craik
Lanarkshire Constabulary

12 September 1932

Police Constable Sydney Hussey Craik chased a suspected illegal bookmaker in the town of Cambuslang on 6 September 1932. The police officer ran across the road at Silverbanks when a passing bus struck him. The constable received injuries to the head and legs and died six days later in Glasgow Royal Infirmary. The police officer came from Carnoustie where his father had been a long-serving police inspector.

IX
Police Constable MacGregor Walker
Dundee City Police

16 September 1932

On 10 September 1932, Police Constables MacGregor Walker and William Nicolson were stopping and checking the driving licences and registration plates of cars on Arbroath Road, Dundee. Nicolson, in uniform, stopped the oncoming cars and Walker, in plainclothes, checked the plates at the front and rear of the vehicles. When Walker was checking the rear plates on a car, an oncoming vehicle rammed into the back of it. The collision trapped the police constable between the cars. Nicolson, although also injured in the crash, arranged for someone to call the emergency services. They arrived at the scene and took the severely injured police officer to hospital. Constable

MacGregor Walker died six days later. The police arrested the drunk driver of the speeding car, twenty-nine-year-old David Halley and charged him with culpable homicide.

At his trial in the High Court at Dundee on 15 January 1933, Halley pled not guilty to the charge of driving a motor car while under the influence of drink to such an extent as to be incapable of having proper control and in a culpable and reckless manner.

Witness Sergeant MacFarland produced a half bottle of whisky that the police found on the passenger seat. The witness, when pressed, admitted the bottle to be untouched and the seal unbroken. Constable Walker had time to give a statement before he died, which the prosecution read to the court: '*The car had ample time to swerve clear of me and Constable Nicolson and reduce speed*'. Dr Young, a police surgeon, said in a statement that when asked to stand on one leg, the accused could not. In Dr Young's opinion the accused was in an unfit state to drive a car at the time of the crash. Inspector William McWalter was present when Dr Young examined the driver and stated that at the police station Halley staggered about and clutched hold of the mantelpiece to steady himself.

Nicolson gave evidence telling the court that he and Walker stopped a Morris car at 11.20pm on Saturday, 10 September. While Nicolson checked the driver's licence, Walker went to the back of the vehicle to inspect the licence plate. The witness said that as he spoke to the driver of the Morris, he became aware of headlights and then a crash which threw him onto the road and underneath the Morris. Nicolson told of getting up and going round to the back of the car to see Constable Walker lying on his back underneath the car that had hit them, his legs protruding. Nicolson said that after the accident, the accused stood half sitting and half standing on the wing of his vehicle, offering no assistance. When told to come to the station, Halley replied, '*We will drive along in my car*'. The police officer grabbed his arm responding, '*You will come with me*'. The witness said just after the collision that Halley smelt strongly of drink, and his eyes were glazed. When asked if Halley realised what had just happened regarding the crash, Nicolson answered, '*He did not*'.

William Campbell witnessed the crash and told the court:

Constable Walker was in a stooping position at the rear of the car when another car drove at a very fast speed. It was on the correct side of the road and the lights were on. Constable Walker held up his hands for the car to stop. The car never slackened speed and no effort was made to steer it away from the stationary car.

Two eyewitnesses to the collision, MacGregor Mitchell and George Raeburn, said that Halley tried to blame the crash on the taillights on the Morris being off. When Halley said to Raeburn immediately after the accident that the lights on the back of the Morris were not burning [on], Raeburn said to Halley, '*Don't come that stuff. The light was burning*'. Another witness at the scene said that Halley smelt of intoxicating liquor.

The question of the rear lights and if they were on or off got even more confused when witness Robert Mackie Watt stated that although he did not see the accident, he passed Constable Walker when the police officer was bent down looking at the back of the Morris. Watt thought that the police officer looked for a considerable time at the rear of the car. The defence put to the jury, either the taillights were not working correctly, or the police officer, in standing behind the vehicle, obstructed the lights.

The defence brought witnesses who did not consider the accused to have been drunk. Jessie Will had spoken to the accused at a club she worked in and she did not believe Halley had been drunk. Jane Orr stated she saw the impact between the cars, and she thought Halley swerved to avoid hitting Walker who had moved onto the middle of the road. Halley swerved towards the kerb to avoid hitting the police officer – the approaching driver would not have hit him if he had not stepped back to the right.

Orr told the court that just after the accident, Halley took out a cushion from his car and placed it under the head of the injured police officer. Orr spoke to the accused and did not consider him to have been drunk.

David Halley gave his evidence and stated that on the afternoon of 10 September, he played golf. After the game, he had his tea in the pavilion along with a pint of beer and later that night, at 7pm, he met a friend in a hotel where he had a small whisky. The two men had a meal and then another small whisky.

Halley then went to the dancing at the New Palais club in South Tay Street. At the club, he met a young lady and took her for a drive. The accused reported that as he drove along Arbroath Road at the junction with Dalkeith Road, he saw a dark coloured stationary car. There was a dark figure to the right of the car in the middle of the road. Halley only had seconds to avoid hitting the man and swerved to the left, but the man jumped back in front. Halley swerved to the right, but it was too late, and the man was caught between the cars.

On 18 January 1933, after a trial which lasted for three days, the jury retired. They returned within the hour with a verdict of guilty to culpable homicide. The judge sentenced David Halley to eighteen-months' imprisonment and a £500 fine. He also suspended his driving licence for four years.

Constable MacGregor Walker's funeral on 19 September 1932 is worth mentioning: Thousands of people stood along the streets between his home at 7 Eden Street and the graveyard. White gloved constables lined the street opposite his home. The funeral party made its way along Arbroath Road and the silent crowd stood four-to-five deep. Factory girls left their work to stand and pay their respects. Shops had closed, and houses had their curtains or blinds drawn, the custom until recently in Scotland. A tramcar stopped whereupon the driver and conductor stood bareheaded to attention as the procession passed. When the party arrived at Dundee's Balgay Cemetery, the police pipe band struck up 'Flowers o' the Forest' and later when the crowd left the cemetery, the band played 'Lochaber No More' as 1,500 mourners made their way out of the graveyard. The size of the funeral provides a good indication as to the popularity and respect held for Constable MacGregor Walker in the city of Dundee at the time of his death.

X

Railway Policemen David Tanner Murdoch and Allan Proudfoot

London Midland & Scottish Railway Police

14 December 1938

A railway police officer walked along the train line between Cowlairs and Port Dundas, Glasgow. The officer could see the grisly remains of something or someone lying between the tracks a short distance from Sighthill goods station at Springburn. The officer switched on his torch and to his horror he recognised the body parts to be two of his colleagues, Railway Policemen David Tanner Murdoch and Allan Proudfoot.

After a series of break-ins in the goods yard, both officers, in plainclothes, patrolled the area. Whilst on patrol, they were hit by a passing train. They lay on the tracks where another train ran over the bodies.

An engine fitter reported that during an inspection of a pilot engine he found traces of blood on the wheels. The driver of that train used to shunt carriages around the yard and told that while pulling fourteen wagons he felt a jolt before a bridge at 8.05pm that night. He thought the guard had applied the brake and he did not see anything unusual.

A public inquiry held in Glasgow returned with a verdict of death by fatal accident.

XI

Special Constable George Lambert Storrar

Fife County Constabulary

23 January 1941

On 23 January 1941, a mine at sea drifted towards the Fife coastal village of West Wemyss. Five men attempted to stop the mine from reaching the small port because if it hit any boats in the harbour or shipping in the Firth of Forth, it could have resulted in a severe loss of life. As the men grappled with the mine, it exploded and killed three of them outright.

Peter Graham was the youngest killed. The sparse report in the *Fife Free Press & Kirkcaldy Guardian* gave Peter's age as sixteen while other accounts claimed he was fifteen. Whatever his age, it is clear young Peter was brave that fateful day. The other dead were David Laing, a seventy-year-old retired miner and Special Constable George Storrar, a thirty-eight-year-old miner and pithead worker. Surviving the explosion, fifty-two-year-old miner James Anderson died later that day. The fifth victim, thirty-seven-year-old Colin Smart, received terrible injuries and died in the first week in February.

XII
Constable Robert Stirrat
Dundee City Police

---

5 May 1941

A message of a strange object lying on the beach at Broughty Ferry arrived at a Dundee Police Station. The police sent Constable Robert Stirrat to investigate. He walked towards the object and we will never know what exactly happened but what is clear is this that the mystery object was a form of ordnance, which subsequently exploded. The blast hurled Stirrat into the air. The police officer lost his right arm and both his legs below the knee. The explosion shattered the windows of nearby houses looking over the beach. Constable Robert Stirrat later died from his wounds in Dundee Royal Infirmary.

XIII
Special Constable David Thompson
Fife Constabulary

12 January 1942

Blacksmith David Thompson liked to do his bit, especially with the war on. A special constable since 1936, the fifty-two-year-old founder member and captain of Strathmiglo cricket team stood to direct traffic on a cold dark night in January 1942. It may be that the police officer stood thinking about how the war had progressed during the quiet spells in between approaching vehicles, or he might have cast his mind back to the weekend when his son had married in the village of Falkland. As the constable stood at the Strathmiglo-Abernethy-Gateside crossroads, an oncoming vehicle hit him. David Thompson died at home from head injuries.

PART SIX

Confronting the 'Supernatural'

The police are required to patrol in the dead of night in dark deserted streets. Often done alone and on foot, this has led to strange reports by patrolling police officers of encounters with 'supernatural' entities.

———————

I
Ghostbusting in Irvine

1878

In September 1878, Constable McGavin was credited in newspaper reports with catching a ghost in Irvine. Rumours of ghostly happenings during the night at Irvine's Trinity Church spread around the North Ayrshire town. On the night of 14 September, a strange otherworldly light was seen among the church's arches facing the river. A large crowd of people stood in shocked amazement watching what was described as a weird and lurid light.

McGavin was not sure that what he witnessed at the church could be considered a supernatural phenomenon and investigated further. Subsequently, the officer caught a man acting suspiciously near the church and took him to Irvine Police Station. Upon investigation, McGavin discovered this man worked as a chemist; he lived near the religious building and wanted to disperse the growing crowds who hoped to witness a paranormal event. To scare the public away, the chemist had placed a saucer with a quantity of phosphorus mixed with other chemicals.

The mixture caused a bright flickering light to dance around the church. Of course, this only brought more ghost hunters and thrill seekers to the area. The police released the chemist without charge, the mystery of the ghost seen in and around the church remained unsolved.

———————

II
Terrified Soldiers Glencorse
Midlothian

1889

Glencorse Barracks, which lies just outside the Midlothian Town of Penicuik, can be an eerie place at night. The old barracks built to house French prisoners of war during the Napoleonic Wars have stories to tell.

In the early hours of 28 November 1889, a sentry in the barracks experienced something 'supernatural'. The event scared him so much, according to *The Dundee Courier* of 30 November 1889, that the sentry had been in a swoon for several hours. The barracks had been the centre of strange paranormal happenings on previous nights.

The next night, another sentry had received such a fright he had deserted his post. The terrified soldier stated something unseen in the darkness had threatened him.

Usually, these frightened men would be the butt of merciless mickey-taking by their comrades. This time, a general feeling of uneasiness spread through the regiment in the barracks; *The Dundee Courier* described the troops as panic-stricken.

The commanding officers gave the soldiers on guard duty at night-time permission to use the bayonet on anything human or supernatural that refused to answer when challenged. The commanders thought the order would put off any hoaxer conducting a practical joke on the sentries. The next night one of the sentries on duty did not appear in the guardroom when expected. A party of soldiers sent to look for the missing man found him slumped over his rifle unconscious. Taken to the hospital, the soldier told of fainting after a ghost had presented a revolver at his head. The military did a full investigation into the Glencorse Barracks haunting.

The inquiry discovered the local police who patrolled around the barracks were fed up with a new young constable who knew it all. The older men, knowing the area around Glencorse to be dark, lacking in streetlamps and a place where spiritual manifestations might be expected by anyone who was superstitious *resolved* to frighten the boasting young police constable. The older officers made noises outside the barracks and played pranks on their young colleague. This had scared the troops within the military compound. The police activity, along with the soldiers' heightened fearful imaginations while on sentry duty, had led to the exaggerated stories of ghosts and hauntings at Glencorse.

III
Capturing a 'Small Ghost'
Gourock

1930

Gourock had two supernatural entities scaring the townspeople in March 1930. The one which haunted the Cardwell Bay district was described as a small figure dressed in white that looked like a wicked little hunchback. The other, a ghost haunting Cloch Road was known to let out low mournful tones.

In the first case, a man returning from a dance saw a white figure that he thought looked decidedly eerie. According to reports he had seen a small apparition:

The figure which was rather small seemed to be clothed in a long flowing garment. Suddenly it seemed to cast its gaze in my direction, gave one long, drawn-out yell, and disappeared around a corner.

The witness stated that when he got to the corner, the ghost had vanished. He added that he thought that someone was playing a practical joke on him. The ghost continued to haunt the area. Locals soon became scared to venture outside in the dark.

Reports proliferated that milk bottles left in the early hours of the morning were disappearing from doorsteps. Believing the missing milk and ghost sightings might be linked, the police kept a watch on the area. Early one morning, a small white figure walked slowly towards a house in Cardwell Road. This 'spook' proceeded to steal the milk at the front door. When the watching officers grabbed the ghost, they discovered it to be a thirteen-year-old boy dressed in a woman's nightdress. The boy used the guise of a restless spirit to scare off anyone in the area so he could steal milk, using the ghostly sightings in Gourock and the inhabitants' uneasiness and fears to his criminal advantage. The young thief appeared at Gourock police court where he received a five-year sentence to be undertaken at Kibble Reformatory, near Paisley.

As for the other restless spirit, a group of youths spent the night in Cloch Road to solve the mystery. They kept watch over the road from their hiding place among a stand of bushes. They all heard the strange moaning sound but did not see anything of note. They did, however, get the fright of their lives when an owl screeched directly above them. Later, upon hearing a purring sound come along the road, they gave a man riding a motorcycle a terrible shock. They jumped from the bushes and emerged in front of the motorcyclist. The youngsters retired at about 2am still unable to find the source of the low mournful moaning.

Sources

NATIONAL RECORDS OF SCOTLAND

JC26/1846/432, JC/1846/433. JC/1846/450 AD14/58/405

JC26/1879

JC 26/1893

BOOKS

David Daiches, *Glasgow* (Bungay: 1977)

Kenneth J Logue, *Popular Disturbances in Scotland 1780–1815* (Edinburgh: 1979)

John Born McGowan, *Policing the Metropolis of Scotland, A History of the Police and Systems of Police in Edinburgh and Edinburghshire 1770–1833* (Musselburgh: 1988)

Gerard Noonan, *The IRA in Britain 1919–1923: 'In the Heart of Enemy Lines'* (Liverpool: 2014)

Alex F Young, *The Encyclopaedia of Scottish Executions 1750 to 1963* (Orpington: 1998)

NEWSPAPERS

Aberdeen Evening Express – 20 July 1942

Aberdeen People's Journal – 24 December 1898

Aberdeen Press and Journal – 4 January 1832, 4 November 1835, 17 September 1878, 18 June 1881, 20 July 1903, 23 March 1904, 24 March 1904, 3 February 1919, 19 April 1919, 5 May 1921, 1 January 1932, 2 January 1932, 6 May 1941

The Airdrie & Coatbridge Advertiser – 25 July 1903

The Ayrshire Express – 7 November 1863

The Banffshire Advertiser – 1 June 1905

The Banffshire Journal and General Advertiser – 23 July 1878,
17 September 1878

The Berwickshire News and General Advertiser – 4 September 1906

The Caledonian Mercury – 21 March 1812, 2 April 1812, 2 May
1812, 3 August 1820, 9 November 1820, 14 December 1820,
16 July 1831, 29 December 1831, 19 March 1840, 25 June
1846, 29 June 1846, 16 June 1858

The Carluke and Lanark Gazette – September 1952

The Coventry Evening Telegraph – 5 September 1952

The Daily Mirror – September 1952

The Daily Record – 6 May 1941

The Daily Review – 6 November 1863, 14 June 1881, 24 June 1882

The Dumfries and Galloway Standard – 15 April 1846

The Dundee Advertiser – 1 September 1896, 24 December 1898

The Dundee Courier – 25 June 1851, 22 October 1851,
4 January 1869, 19 September 1870, 21 September 1870,
29 September 1870, 7 May 1875, 15 October 1877,
1 November 1878, 14 June 1881, 19 June 1882,
6 September 1883, 18 March 1885, 12 September 1892,
15 April 1893, 16 August 1893, 25 March 1896,
15 February 1899, 30 November 1889, 25 July 1905,
3 June 1908, 20 January 1919, 1 February 1919, 2 May 1921,
27 August 1926, 29 August 1926, 19 October 1926,
2 January 1932, 20 September 1932, 6 May 1941,
14 January 1942, 16 January 1942, 23 May 1951, 25 July 1951,
26 July 1951, 27 July 1951, 28 July 1951, 26 September 1951,
26 November 1952

The Dundee Evening Telegraph – 14 September 1878,
16 August 1893, 23 June 1897, 5 April 1900, 19 November 1901,

27 May 1905, 2 June 1919, 29 October 1920, 8 February 1921,
5 May 1921, 11 May 1921, 26 October 1921, 27 October 1921,
27 August 1926, 18 January 1933

The Dundee, Perth, and Cupar Advertiser – 9 May 1848,
24 June 1851,17 October 1851

The Dundee People's Journal, 15 March 1930

The Edinburgh Evening Courant – 2 December 1868,
2 February 1869

The Edinburgh Evening News – 17 September 1878,
15 March 1881, 8 July 1886, 15 October 1892, 23 March 1896,
20 April 1896, 4 April 1900, 5 April 1900, 30 August 1906,
6 August 1921, 17 September 1932, 17 January 1933

The Edinburgh Evening Post and Scottish Standard – 4 March 1846

The Elgin Courier – 6 March 1846

The Falkirk Herald – 3 June 1888, 22 April 1896, 16 May 1896,
20 January 1923

The Fife Free Press & Kirkcaldy Guardian – 26 May 1883,
2 July 1883, 7 July 1883, 25 January 1919, 7 May 1921,
25 January 1941

The Fife Herald – 9 May 1844, 7 November 1878

The Fifeshire Advertiser – 24 June 1882

The Forfar Herald – 11 August 1905

Forward – 14 June 1919

The Glasgow Evening Citizen – 21 April 1869

The Glasgow Evening Post – 15 March 1881, 9 September 1893,
30 October 1893

The Glasgow Herald – 29 January 1844, 29 August 1853,
21 July 1858, 13 June 1881,11 October 1883, 16 August 1893,
6 September 1893, 11 September 1893, 31 October 1893,
1 September 1896, 26 September 1896, 25 October 1897,
26 October 1897, 20 November 1897, 22 December 1898

Glasgow Morning Journal – 29 August 1865

The Greenock Telegraph and Clyde Shipping Gazette – 28 August 1906

The Hawick Express – 19 January 1933

The Hartlepool Northern Daily Mail – 14 December 1938

The Illustrated Police News – 31 December 1898

The Inverness Courier – 10 August 1820, 11 March 1846,
14 March 1848, 25 July 1878, 19 September 1878

The Jedburgh Gazette – 1 September 1906

The Leith Burghs Pilot – 24 June 1882

The Military Register – 10 December 1820

*The Montrose, Arbroath and Brechin Review and Forfar and
Kincardineshire Advertiser* – 27 June 1851,

The Motherwell Times – 23 June 1888, 17 December 1920,
28 January 1921

The North British Agriculturist – 28 April 1869

The North British Daily Mail – 1 June 1858

The Northern Scot and Moray & Nairn Express – 19 August 1893

The Orcadian – 26 July 1858

The Paisley Herald and Renfrewshire Advertiser – 26 December 1863

The Perthshire Advertiser – 16 October 1851, 11 October 1895

The Perthshire Courier – 9 January 1812, 26 March 1812,
26 January 1832,

Port-Glasgow Express – 3 June 1908

The Portsmouth Evening News – 15 September 1951

The Renfrewshire Independent – 9 January 1869

The Royal Cornwall Gazette 1– 2 August 1820, 4 February 1832

The Scotsman – 27 July 1831, 18 November 1868,
2 February 1869, 14 September 1878, 19 June 1882,
23 June 1882, 24 June 1882, 26 June 1882, 29 October 1920,
9 February 1921, 10 February 1921, 10 August 1921,

11 August 1921, 12 August 1921, 13 August 1921,
15 August 1921, 16 August 1921, 17 August 1921,
18 August 1921, 19 August 1921, 20 August 1921,
22 August 1921, 17 January 1933, 18 January 1933,
15 December 1938, 28 December 1938, 18 September 1940,
19 September 1940, 4 April 1942,

The Sheffield Independent – 1 February 1919

The Sunday Post – 8 May 1921,7 August 1921, 29 August 1926

The Southern Reporter – 7 November 1878, 15 September 1892

The Western Daily Press – 21 April 1923

The Western Mail – 6 September 1952

The Western Times – 29 August 1906

The Wishaw Press – 16 September 1932

The Witness – 21 March 1840, 1 April 1846,

The Worcestershire Chronicle – 25 April 1896

MAGAZINES

The Scots Magazine – 1 January 1812

WEBSITES

british-police-history.uk
policemuseum.org.uk
www.aberdeen.gov.uk
www.btphg.org.uk
www.lphs.org.uk
www.spmt.scot

About the Author

Gary Knight is a renowned historical storyteller and tour guide with a passion for history, a talent for storytelling and in interest in Scotland's dark and dangerous past. He has worked throughout Scotland and appeared on television and radio with his company History and Horror Tours. You can catch up with Gary on his nighttime walking tours: www.historyandhorrortours.com.

This is Gary's second book. His first, *No Fair City: Dark Tales from Perth's Past*, was published in 2017 and has been described as 'hard to put down'. Gary's third book is very much under wraps for now.

TIPPERMUIR BOOKS

Tippermuir Books Ltd (est. 2009) is an independent publishing company based in Perth, Scotland.

PUBLISHING HISTORY

Spanish Thermopylae (2009)

Battleground Perthshire (2009)

Perth: Street by Street (2012)

Born in Perthshire (2012)

In Spain with Orwell (2013)

Trust (2014)

Perth: As Others Saw Us (2014)

Love All (2015)

A Chocolate Soldier (2016)

The Early Photographers of Perthshire (2016)

Taking Detective Novels Seriously: The Collected Crime Reviews of Dorothy L Sayers (2017)

Walking with Ghosts (2017)

No Fair City: Dark Tales from Perth's Past (2017)

The Tale o the Wee Mowdie that wantit tae ken wha keeched on his heid (2017)

Hunters: Wee Stories from the Crescent: A Reminiscence of Perth's Hunter Crescent (2017)

A Little Book of Carol's (2018)

Flipstones (2018)

Perth: Scott's Fair City:
The Fair Maid of Perth & Sir Walter Scott –
A Celebration & Guided Tour (2018)

God, Hitler, and Lord Peter Wimsey: Selected Essays,
Speeches and Articles by Dorothy L Sayers (2019)

Perth & Kinross: A Pocket Miscellany:
A Companion for Visitors and Residents (2019)

The Piper of Tobruk:
Pipe Major Robert Roy, MBE, DCM (2019)

The 'Gig Docter o Athole':
Dr William Irvine & The Irvine Memorial Hospital (2019)

Afore the Highlands: The Jacobites in Perth, 1715–16 (2019)

'Where Sky and Summit Meet':
Flight Over Perthshire – A History: Tales of Pilots,
Airfields, Aeronautical Feats, & War (2019)

Diverted Traffic (2020)

Authentic Democracy:
An Ethical Justification of Anarchism (2020)

'If Rivers Could Sing': A Scottish River Wildlife Journey.
A Year in the Life of the River Devon as it flows
through the Counties of Perthshire,
Kinross-shire & Clackmannanshire (2020)

A Squatter o Bairnrhymes (2020)

In a Sma Room Songbook:
From the Poems by William Soutar
(2020)

The Nicht Afore Christmas:
The much-loved yuletide tale in Scots (2020)

Ice Cold Blood (eBook, 2021)

The Perth Riverside Nursery & Beyond:
A Spirit of Enterprise and Improvement
(Elspeth Bruce and Pat Kerr, 2021)

The Shanter Legacy:
The Search for the Grey Mare's Tail
(Garry Stewart, 2021)

FORTHCOMING

William Soutar: Collected Poetry, Volume I
(Published Work)
(Kirsteen McCue and Paul S Philippou (editors), 2021)

William Soutar: Collected Poetry, Volume II
(Unpublished Work)
(Kirsteen McCue and Paul S Philippou (editors), 2022)

A Scottish Wildlife Odyssey (Keith Broomfield, 2021)

Beyond the Swelkie:
A Collection of New Poems and Writings to Mark the
Centenary of George Mackay Brown (1921–1996)
(Jim Mackintosh & Paul S Philippou (editors), 2021)

All Tippermuir Books titles are
available from bookshops and online booksellers.
They can also be purchased directly
with free postage & packing [UK only] –
(minimum charges for overseas delivery) from

www.tippermuirbooks.co.uk

Tippermuir Books Ltd can be contacted at
mail@tippermuirbooks.co.uk

Lullaby
Press

TIPPERMUIR
· BOOKS LIMITED ·